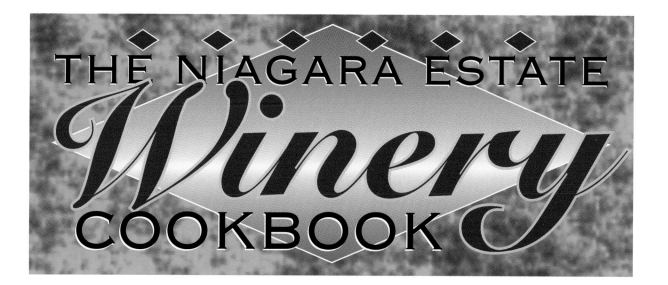

THE NIAGARA ESTATE *Winery* COOKBOOK

JAMES BRUCE
PHOTOGRAPHY BY DIETER HESSEL

◆ ◆ ◆ ◆ ◆ ◆

W
Warwick Publishing Inc.
Toronto   Los Angeles

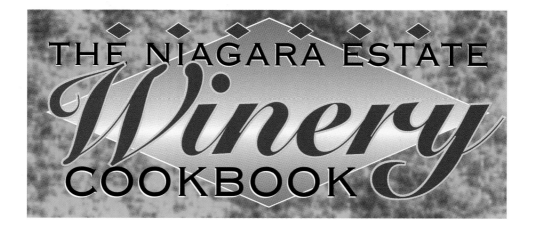

THE NIAGARA ESTATE
Winery
COOKBOOK

ISBN 1-895629-31-4

Published by Warwick publishing Inc. 24 Mercer Street, Toronto, Ontario M5V 1H3

Distributed to the book trade by:
Firefly Books Ltd.
250 Sparks Ave,
Willowdale, Ontario
M2H 2S4

Printed and bound in Canada by Metropole Litho Inc.

To my children Robbie, Ann, Charlton, and James
for their understanding and support.
— J.B.

To wine makers and chefs around the world
who make dining a delight.
— D.H.

ACKNOWLEDGEMENTS

I would like to offer my appreciation and thanks, in no particular order, to: Lynn, Joyce and George Osmond for introducing me to Niagara and for making me aware of the wide variety of local produce through wonderful, home-cooked dinners; Debi Pratt of Inniskillin, for her encouragement and guidance from the beginning; Peter Gamble of the VQA, for providing information and for his personal support; the winemakers, winery owners and staffs who were so cooperative in helping to produce the book, in particular those who constantly worked with us in arranging photography and providing information: John DeSousa Jr. of DeSousa Wine Cellars; Lorraine Gurinskas of Lakeview Cellars Estate Winery; Allan Schmidt of Vineland Estates Wines; Leonard and Tom Pennachetti of Cave Spring; Paul Speck of Henry of Pelham Estate Winery; Paul Bosc Jr. and Rolph Lutz of Château des Charmes; Greg Berti of Hillebrand Estates Winery; Rick Hunse of Stonechurch Vineyards; Gudrun Konzelmann of Konzelmann Winery & Vineyards; Sabina Reif of Reif Estate Winery; Donald Ziraldo of Inniskillin Wines; John and Sandra Marynissen of Marynissen Estates; Jim Warren of Stoney Ridge Cellars; Charles Pillitteri and Heather Brinsmead of Pillitteri Estates Winery; Angel Hernder of Hernder Estate Wines; the professional chefs who contributed their time to cook and prepare wonderful presentations, and to painstakingly prepare the recipes: Jamie Kennedy, Emil Rinderlin, Graeme Gatenby-Wilson, Michael Olson, Izabela Kalabis, Mark Walpole, Barry Burton, Michael Städtlander, Marc Thuet, Keith Froggett, Gabriel DeFrietas, Greg Willis, Tony Nuth, Ralph Bretzigheimer, and food consultant Barbara Groen; the celebrity chefs who contributed their valuable time to cook and prepare wonderful presentations, and to prepare recipes: Andy Brandt, Christopher Newton, Trisha Romance, and Jonathan Welsh;

Carolyn and Peter Hubbard, and Jim Henderson, for helping with recipe copy; photographer Dieter Hessel for his wonderful work and professionalism; Nick Pitt of Warwick publishing for his support and patience during the past many months; Jim Williamson of Warwick Publishing who had the vision to produce this book; and Lee Hornberger, Doug Wilson and Liz Watkinson for "being there."

CONTENTS

VINTNERS QUALITY ALLIANCE (VQA)

The VQA plays an important role in wine selection by consumers. Peter Gamble, Executive Director of the VQA, explains why the system exists and how it works.

Every wine growing country in the world has a set of standards for its finest products. They enable consumers, through a distinctive designation on each bottle, to identify easily those wines of superior quality and their viticultural area of origin.

Each country has a different name for its controlling regulatory body. In Canada, the Vintners Quality Alliance (VQA) sets the standards.

It is a voluntary, independent alliance of representatives of various groups, including representatives from industry, government, hospitality and academic communities. The standards are precise. They identify the geographical areas in the country where grapes can be grown and how the wine must be produced. They also stipulate which varieties of grapes can be used to produce superior products carrying the VQA medallion. Canada has three distinct wine growing regions, the provinces of British Columbia, Nova Scotia and Ontario. In Ontario, Niagara is one of three Designated Viticultural Areas which have traditionally produced the finest and most distinctive wines. The other two are Pelee Island and Lake Erie North Shore.

Wines bearing the VQA medallion must have met stringent production and appellation standards and have been approved by a panel of experts. In Ontario, all VQA wines must be made from 100 percent Ontario grapes. These grapes must be the classic European varieties such as Chardonnay, Cabernet Sauvignon, Riesling and Pinot Noir. The most coveted VQA medallion is the black on gold seal. The judging standard is so stringent for this award that only about three percent of VQA wines receive it.

Apart from providing an important identification system for consumers, the VQA also ensures that the wines continue to live up to the high standards set by the alliance.

INTRODUCTION

In the heart of Niagara is Niagara-On-The-Lake, one of the prettiest towns anywhere and steeped in history and culture. It's where Upper Canada began in 1792, and was then known as Newark. For more than 30 years it has been home to the internationally renowned Shaw Festival. Nestled on the shore of Lake Ontario, it reminds me of my hometown in Scotland with its old inns that serve afternoon tea, its Queen Street with quaint shops, its beautiful gardens and parks, and the local golf course on the lake that stays open all year.

Now Niagara-On-The-Lake is fast becoming recognized around the world as home to several international award winning wineries, and in the midst of a wine growing area that is seeing explosive growth.

This area, located between Lake Ontario and the Niagara Escarpment, has an ideal mix of soil and minerals for growing the classic wine grapes of Europe and producing equally superb wines. And the combination of the sheltering effect of the Escarpment and the moderating influence of the Lake create a micro-climate which helps to protect the vines. It's interesting to note that the Niagara wine region is slightly south of Burgundy, France.

The fact that the Niagara estate wineries have been upstaging many of the traditional old world wine growing countries by winning significant numbers of awards at European wine competitions is a sweet reward for the Niagara winemakers. It has been a difficult, uphill battle. The entrepreneurial owners, particularly those who started the fledgling industry, faced tremendous adversity and through hard work, dedication to quality, and vision have now taken their place on the international wine scene. Each of the wineries has an interesting, personal history. Some of the wine making families have heritages that go back many generations in the old world wine growing regions. Others had family fruit farms in Niagara and, years ago, recognized the potential of the industry. All have one important goal in common. As estate wineries, each wants to produce the best quality wines possible, and each is constantly experimenting to further improve the excellent wines they already produce and to introduce new products to the fortunate consumer.

There is no arrogance amongst this group. Everyone connected with the wineries in Niagara are pleased and delighted to help visitors make wine tasting a pleasurable experience. They want visitors to share their love of wines. Their openness and desire to educate are evident through their educational tours and tastings at the individual wineries.

There is no greater recognition for the excellent wines being produced in Niagara than by another group of artists in this book, some of the best chefs in Canada. The fact that these chefs are pleased to have Niagara wines complement their meals is a tribute to the winemakers. Each chef I approached was delighted to match up with a winery and the wonderful, interesting recipes reflect each chef's own artistry. I must point out that the chefs work on a regular basis with a number of these wineries, not just the one each is matched with in this book. Where possible, based on freshness and diversity, the chefs often use local produce and game to create a cuisine which is becoming unique to the province of Ontario.

Three of the celebrity chefs in the book represent the cultural community which plays such an important role in Niagara. Christopher Newton, the artistic director; Tricia Romance, the artist; and Jonathan Welsh, the actor, all have ties to the community. And Andy Brandt has played a very significant role in supporting and promoting the wine industry in Niagara and other parts of Ontario.

Although this book is about the Niagara estate wineries, there are other excellent larger wineries in Niagara and small, fine wineries in two other traditional wine growing areas in Ontario, Pelee Island and Lake Erie North Shore.

In choosing wine with food, there are no longer any hard and fast rules. There are only some basic principles that will enhance your love of particular wines with certain foods. Otherwise, personal taste should ultimately be your guide.

Hopefully most of the wines photographed and mentioned in this book will be available, though some may not. In that case, the individual winery will be able to recommend a similar wine as a substitute.

Although we have tried to make sure the recipes are within the capability of the average cook, some require preparation a day in advance or take some extra time. They're great for entertaining. But there are also a number of easier dishes and you may, in fact, want to mix and match some of the recipes. In some cases, you don't have to make a particular sauce to enjoy the food.

Let your imagination work as you view the photographs of the wineries and the food. You're in for a delectable time.

A Local Dinner at the Winery Restaurant

CAVE SPRING CELLARS

In the Old World, as Leonard Pennachetti carefully explains, it has long been known that the best vineyards are situated on hillsides. He believes Cave Spring Cellars wines are unique, because they capture the *goût de terroir*, or "taste of the soil" produced from grapes grown on the Beamsville Bench. This narrow finger of land running along the hillside of the Niagara Escarpment possesses well-drained, mineral rich soils ideal for grape growing. As well, the Bench's proximity to Lake Ontario helps to moderate winter and summer temperatures. With these factors and the optimal air flow patterns on the hillside, the Beamsville Bench has all the ingredients for producing superb wines.

As a youngster growing up in the area, Leonard had a keen interest in grapes. His grandfather, Giuseppe Pennachetti, an immigrant from the Marché region of Italy, regularly took Leonard along with him to care for a family vineyard near St. Catharines, Ontario. In 1974, Leonard and his father, John, prepared a 12 acre parcel of land for plantings of Riesling and Chardonnay. These vines were among the first *vitis*

vinifera varieties planted in Ontario. Today, Cave Spring Cellars remains committed to using exclusively *vitis vinifera* grape varieties. As a result of their success, there have been several new plantings. The winery now owns about 33 acres of vineyards with plans for extensive plantings over the next few years.

The winery is in an historic building dating back to 1871 in the charming village of Jordan. The village's main street is lined with a number of quaint antique, stained glass, art, and gift stores. The winery building itself is home to the Cave Spring retail store, an antique centre where several area dealers display their antiques for sale, as well as other handcraft and gift shops, and On The Twenty, Ontario's first winery restaurant. Named for its picturesque view of the Twenty Mile Creek, the restaurant has enjoyed critical acclaim for its relaxed, yet elegant, atmosphere filled with foliage, fresh flowers and baskets of fruit.

Using local produce and regional cuisine, Chef Michael Olson offers a wide variety of dishes including roasted Beamsville chicken breast, Speck farm quails on Indian

Summer Riesling butter, fresh trout from nearby Shorthills farm in honey mustard glaze, and cinnamon cured Smithville duck breast. Each day Michael visits his local suppliers to choose the best seasonal produce. Those eating at On The Twenty on a particular day might be fortunate enough to be offered local smoked trout with red radish relish, corn-sweet pepper soup or breast of guinea fowl and oishi plum blackberry coulis.

Leonard Pennachetti is now as proud of his restaurant as he is of Cave Spring's high quality, award winning wines. At the 1994 prestigious VinItaly international wine competition in Verona, Italy, Cave Spring won the Grand Gold for their 1991 Chardonnay Reserve. This is the highest award in a competition that involves 16 countries and more than 900 wineries. Many of their wines are blended from grapes grown on the Cave Spring farm and other carefully selected vineyards along the Beamsville Bench. By blending fruit from different vineyards, the winemakers at Cave Spring Cellars are able to produce excellent wines with remarkable consistency.

Cave Spring Cellars has also played an important role at the forefront of the Ontario wine industry's commitment to quality through its founding membership in the Vintners Quality Alliance (VQA).

🐉 MENU 🐉

Chardonnay Smoked Shorthills Trout with Beetroot Horseradish and Hothouse Greens
Cave Spring Cellars 1992 Riesling Reserve

Cinnamon Scented Smithville Duck Breast in Ginger-Black Currant Pan Juices
Cave Spring Cellars 1992 Cabernet Merlot

Whistle Hill Matsu Apple and Tavistock Cheddar Pie on Riesling Sabayon
Cave Spring Cellars Indian Summer Riesling

Chardonnay Smoked Shorthills Trout with Beetroot Horseradish and Hothouse Greens

- 4 smoked trout fillets
- 1 bunch of beetroots
- ¼ cup (50 mL) white vinegar
  balsamic vinaigrette
  horseradish
  touch of salt and freshly ground pepper
  a variety of greens
- 1 cup (250 mL) chicken stock
- ¼ cup (50 mL) Chardonnay

For Michael Olson's particular use at On The Twenty Restaurant, the smoked trout fillets are marinated for several hours in a Cave Spring Cellars Chardonnay. He says this process transfers just enough of the flavour he desires so that it is an almost perfect match with a glass of Riesling.

The Beetroot Horseradish is a very simple accompaniment for the trout. Cook the beetroots in a flavourful chicken stock with about ¼ cup (50 mL) of white vinegar to retain the colour, until tender.

Pureé the cooked beets and mix on a 1 to 1 basis with horseradish. Season with freshly ground pepper and a touch of salt. Serve with a light salad of your favorite greens and just a hint of balsamic vinaigrette.

Serves 4

Preparation time is about 30 minutes. To save time, you can marinate the trout fillets overnight in the refrigerator.

Cinnamon Scented Smithville Duck Breast in Ginger–Black Currant Pan Juices

- 1 whole duck
  sugar, coarse salt, and cinnamon
- 1 onion
- 1 celery stalk
- 1 carrot
- ¼ cup (50 g) chopped ginger
- ¼ cup (50 mL) black currants
- 1 tbsp (30 g) butter

Opposite page: *Chardonnay Smoked Shorthills Trout with Beetroot Horseradish and Hothouse Greens*

Left: *Cinnamon Scented Smithville Duck Breast in Ginger–Black Currant Pan Juices*

Remove breasts from the duck and trim fat from breasts, leaving a simple covering. Make diagonal cuts into fat, but not through the meat. Press both sides of breasts onto a mixture of sugar, coarse salt and cinnamon. Allow to sit uncovered for at least two days in refrigerator.

Remove legs from duck. Roast carcass until golden brown. To prepare stock, cut carcass into 3 or 4 pieces. Cover with 9 cups (2 litres) of water and ¼ cup Mecscrement of Cabernet Merlot. Add the onion, celery stalk, and carrot, all roughly cut, and chopped ginger. Reduce this from 9 cups (2 litres) to about 1¼ cups (300 mL). Strain this rich, flavourful stock carefully through cheesecloth or a very fine sieve. Reserve stock.

For cooking duck, it is best to use a cast iron skillet. Heat skillet dry, then add the duck breasts fat side down in the pan. Draining fat every two minutes, continue cooking for about six to eight minutes, to medium rare. Turn the duck onto the meat side of the breast, cook for one minute and remove duck from pan. Reserve.

Add stock to the skillet, deglazing it and enriching it further. Add black currants and quickly heat through, whipping in 1 tbsp (30 g) of butter just before serving. Place duck as thinly as possible and fan out on each plate. Serve sauce over sliced breast.

Serves 2

Prepare breasts and allow to sit for 2 days in refrigerator. Preparation time for stock and cooking is approximately 1 hour.

Whistle Hill Matsu Apple and Tavistock Cheddar Pie on Riesling Sabayon

1¾ cups (400 g) vegetable shortening
2 cups (230 g) flour
⅓ cup (100 g) vinegar, egg, water
1 tsp (5 g) salt

For filling
8 Matsu apples
1 tsp (5 g) cinnamon
grate of nutmeg
⅔ cup (150 g) sugar
2 cups (200 g) shredded cheddar

1 egg yolk
½ cup (100 mL) milk

For sauce
5 egg yolks
⅓ cup (100 g) sugar
1 cup (200 mL) Riesling

Work flour, salt, and shortening together until it crumbles into small pieces the size of garden peas. Add ice cold water, egg, vinegar and work only until it holds together. Refrigerate for 40 minutes.

Peel, core and slice 8 apples, mix with cinnamon, nutmeg and ⅔ cup (150 g) of sugar. Put into lined pastry plate and sprinkle with shredded cheddar. Cover with pastry top, brush with egg yolk mixed with milk and sprinkle lightly with sugar. Bake for 45 minutes at 375F (190°C) until apples are cooked through.

To prepare sauce, whip over a double boiler until frothy (mixture will hold a figure 8 drawn over it) but do not scramble the eggs. Remove from heat and cool by whipping in 1 cup (200 mL) of 18–35% cream. Refrigerate for 30 minutes.

Serves 6 to 8.
Preparation time is approximately 1 hour, not including refrigeration time.

About the Wines

In choosing the 1992 Riesling Reserve with the smoked trout chef Michael Olson explains: "The pear and citrus accents predominate in the wine, complement the flavour and texture of the fresh smoked rainbow trout. The fish is marinated in wine and then slowly smoked over applewood embers infused with vinifera vine trimmings. The full fruit of the Riesling stands up to the smoke of the trout and the acidity of the horseradish compote."

He picked the 1992 Cabernet Merlot with the duck because, he says, "The berry-like tendencies of this wine pair well with full-bodied meats like duck. The wine leans toward bell pepper and light smoke and licorice tones. The duck reflects this with a slight cinnamon scent and ginger-cassis flavours in the sauce."

For the dessert, Michael chose Indian Summer Riesling. "Strong apricot honey scents with a complex acidity make the Indian Summer a complement unlike any other for cooked fruit dessert. The particular apples in this pie are grown on virtually the same soil as the grapes. A simple cardamom sauce widens the apple and wine flavours to round off the dessert."

Top Left: *Winemakers Angelo Pavan and Leonard Pennachetti.*

CHEF MICHAEL OLSON

Before joining Cave Spring's On The Twenty Restaurant in 1993, Michael worked at several restaurants in Toronto and Ottawa. Now he is pleasing customers with imaginatively designed dishes featuring the finest in locally grown products. "Moving to the Niagara Peninsula has opened my eyes to the link between farmer and cook—one that is all too often lost in the modern-day food business."

Michael is a founding member of the Knives and Forks Chef Federation, which promotes the use of organically grown farm produce in Ontario. Michael's mission is to showcase Niagara's produce alongside VQA wines in a relaxed, country setting.

17

A Hearty Dinner in the Château

CHÂTEAU DES CHARMES WINES

The Bosc family has an air of tradition and charm that comes with generations of winemaking experience and international recognition as the owners of one of Canada's finest wineries.

This is a family run winery. The patriarch is Paul Michel Bosc Sr., a fifth generation French grape grower whose ancestors established their own vineyards in Algeria in 1840. Paul followed a long family tradition by studying viticulture and oenology, graduating from the University of Dijon in Burgundy, France. He emigrated to Canada in 1963 and began working as a clerk at a wine store in Montreal. Within a few months he placed a call to a Niagara winery that was having quality control problems. Not only did he inform them of the problem, he told them how to rectify it. They were so impressed an executive from the winery flew to Montreal and hired him. Fifteen years later, in 1978, Paul Bosc founded Château des Charmes.

Paul Bosc is uncompromising when it comes to viticulture and oenology and he maintains an ongoing commitment to research and development. Château des Charmes was the first winery in Canada to establish its own vinifera vineyards and is a leader in developing innovative techniques in viticulture and wine technology. They work almost exclusively with vinifera grapes producing Chardonnay, Pinot Noir, Cabernet Sauvignon, Riesling and Gamay Noir to name a few.

All the members of Paul's family are actively involved in the business. Paul's wife, Andrée, leads very popular tours and tastings. Paul's son, Pierre-Jean, who is also a graduate of the University of Dijon, is oenologist and production manager. Paul Bosc Jr. is director of marketing. Through his efforts and the quality of Château des Charmes wines, the winery was chosen as the exclusive official supplier for Canada's 125th birthday celebrations. He has also spearheaded a successful drive for increased international sales of Ontario wines.

One of the greatest tributes paid to Château des Charmes came in the summer of 1993 at Vin-Expo, the world's most important and largest wine trade fair held biannually in Bordeaux, France. Equivalent to winning an Olympic gold medal, Château des Charmes won a gold medal for their 1990 Paul Bosc Estate Chardonnay. There were 4,080 wines from 26 countries judged by 1250 experts at Vin-Expo. The Chardonnay was the only North American white wine to win a gold medal.

The winery now has a new home, a $6 million French château built in the great tradition of Canada's 19th century hotels like the Château Laurier in Ottawa or the Banff Springs Hotel in Banff, Alberta. A 35,000 square foot facility, the château has a capacity of about 140,000 cases of wine annually. The new winery houses extensive underground cellars, a kitchen and banquet facility and a theatre. Surrounded by 85 acres of new vineyards and planted predominantly with Chardonnay and Pinot Noir, the new Château des Charmes winery stands as an impressive example of the emerging greatness of the Niagara Wine Region.

✂ MENU ✂

Yukon Gold Potato and Parsnip Chowder
Château des Charmes 1991 Gamay Blanc

Roast Cornish Game Hen with Smoked Sausage Stuffing and Dried Cranberries
Château des Charmes 1991 Gamay Noir

Pear Crisp Stuffed with Hazelnuts
Château des Charmes 1990 Late Harvest Riesling

Yukon Gold Potato and Parsnip Chowder

5 slices bacon
1 onion
   all purpose flour, as needed
½ clove garlic
1 lb (450 g) parsnips
1 lb (450 g) potatoes
3 cups (750 mL) chicken stock
3 white peppercorns
2 stems parsley
   pinch thyme
½ bay leaf
½ tsp (2.5 g) caraway seeds
1 cup (250 mL) cream

Finely mince bacon, onion and garlic clove. Peel potatoes and parsnips and dice to one half inch. In a heavy bottom sauce pan, sauté until the fat is rendered and bacon is crispy. Add onion and sauté until translucent or about five minutes. Sprinkle with flour and make a roux and cook for two minutes. Add garlic, potatoes, parsnips and toss briefly. Slowly add chicken stock a little at a time while stirring constantly with a wooden spoon. Bring to a boil, then reduce heat to simmer. Combine herbs in a cheese cloth bag and tie with string, making a sachet, and add to soup. Cook until potatoes and parsnips are tender. Transfer half of the soup to a food processor and purée until smooth, then combine with remaining soup. Add heavy cream and adjust seasoning with salt and white pepper.

To serve, use a warm soup plate. Garnish with chives and sautéed rye bread croutons. Barry Burton likes to garnish with a little sour cream and beet juice mixed together in a squeeze bottle, although this is optional.

Serves 4

Preparation time is approximately 45 minutes.

Roast Cornish Game Hen with Smoked Sausage Stuffing and Dried Cranberries

FOR HENS
4 cornish hens
½ cup (100 mL) melted butter
   salt
   pepper
10 x 2" (5 cm) strips parchment paper or wax paper

FOR STUFFING
2 tbsp (30 mL) butter
2½ cups (575 g) diced cornbread
2 tbsp (30 g) chopped parsley
1 small onion
1 stalk celery
1 tsp (5 g) ground sage
1 tsp (5 g) thyme
1 tsp (5 g) rosemary
⅓ lb (170 g) smoked sausage
¼ cup (50 g) dried cranberries
¼ cup (50 mL) chicken stock
1 egg
   salt

20

freshly ground pepper
½ cup (100 mL) sherry
2 tbsp (30 mL) apple cider

To prepare the cornish game hens, bone the hens by cutting through the wing bones just above the first joint, then cut down the back with a boning knife. With the end of the blade, slowly begin to pull the meat and skin away from the bone, making sure that the meat and skin stay attached. Cut the leg bone at the joint and pull away from the carcass. Repeat this around the breast bone and cut wing bones so the carcass can be removed. Pull the wing bones through the skin and remove. Remove thigh bone and cut at first joint keeping leg bone attached. Season hens with salt and white pepper and reserve.

To prepare the stuffing, which you can do the day before if you wish, finely dice onions, celery and smoke sausage. Soak dried cranberries in a little warm sherry to soften. (In the supermarket, you can sometimes find them under the name Crasins or you can use dried blueberries or other dried fruit as a replacement).

In a heavy bottom pot, melt butter and sauté onions and celery. Cook until translucent or about five minutes. Add sausage, cranberries, thyme, rosemary and sage. Sauté for an additional two minutes. Remove from heat and add chopped parsley, beaten egg and cornbread. (You may have to make your own cornbread. Buy a box of cornmeal and there is a simple recipe on the side). Gently blend together. Add stock and adjust seasoning with salt and freshly ground pepper. Allow to cool.

Place ½ cup (125 g) of stuffing in the centre of hens' breast meat. Pull meat and skin up around stuffing so that stuffing is completely covered. Turn hens over so that breast and legs are facing up. Place hens on a small roast pan. Wrap greased parchment paper strips around the bottom of the hens to make a tight bundle (you can use wax paper instead). Brush hens with melted butter and roast at 375F (190°C) for 30 minutes.

To serve, transfer hens to warm dinner plates. Pour off fat from roast

Opposite page: *Yukon Gold Potato and Parsnip Chowder*

Below: *Roast Cornish Game Hen With Smoked Sausage Stuffing and Dried Cranberries*

pan and add 2 tbsp (30 mL) of sherry, 2 tbsp (30 mL) of apple cider and ¾ cup (175 mL) of chicken stock. Bring to a boil, stirring and scraping the dripping from the pan. Thicken with a little stock and water. Simmer for a few minutes and serve over hens.

Serves 4

Preparation time is about 1½ hours.

Pear Crisp Stuffed with Hazelnuts

1   cup (225 g) sugar
2   cups (500 mL) water
1   tbsp (20 mL) lemon juice
1   tbsp (20 mL) pear liqueur
4   pears
⅓   cup (75 g) hazelnut
    heavy cream, as needed
⅓   cup (75 g) nougatine
2   tbsp (40 g) butter
4   spring roll papers

FOR SAUCE
⅓   cup (75 g) brown sugar
⅓   cup (75 mL) corn syrup
⅓   cup (75 mL) poaching liquid
2   tbsp (40 mL) pear liqueur

    seasonal fruit
    mint sprigs

To prepare the pears, make a simple syrup from the sugar, water, lemon juice and liqueur. Peel the pears with stems attached. Core them using a melon

baller. Poach the pears in the syrup until a knife will easily pierce the centers. Cool them in the liquid, remove and keep at room temperature. Reserve 1/2 cup (100 mL) of the poaching liquid for the sauce. In a mixing bowl, combine the crushed nougatine with a little cream, blend until smooth but still firm and fill the poached pears. Brush the spring roll with a little melted butter, place each pear in the center of each sheet and fold the ends up around the stems in a purse.

For the sauce, in a heavy bottom sauce pan combine the brown sugar, corn syrup, poaching liquid and liqueur.

Bring to a boil, reduce heat and simmer uncovered until slightly thick.

To serve, heat pastry wrapped pears in a microwave oven. Transfer to a paper-lined sheet pan and bake at 350F (180°C) for eight to ten minutes to brown the pastry. Place each pear on a plate and drizzle the warm sauce over the pears, forming a pool of the sauce at the base and garnish with seasonal fruit, mint sprigs and sweetened whipped cream.

Serves 4

Preparation time is approximately 40 minutes.

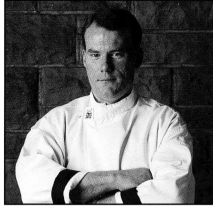

CHEF BARRY BURTON

🜏 About The Wines 🜏

Chef Barry Burton picked the Gamay Blanc with the soup because, as he says, "This wine has a lively acidity, and Gamay Blanc is dry in taste which lends itself well to any chowder or cream based soup. It has a good clean finish."

Barry chose the Gamay Noir with the cornish game hen because this wine is light with a cherry flavour and a nice acidity that blends well with the smoked flavouring of the stuffing and has an excellent finish.

He says that the Late Harvest Riesling matches well with the pear crisp dessert because this wine is fruity flavoured with tastes of pear, apple and honey overtones and a clean finish.

Opposite page: *Pear Crisp stuffed with Hazelnuts*
Above: *The Bosc family, Paul Jr., Paul, Pierre-Jean and Andrée*

Barry began cooking at the age of 16 as an employee of the Niagara Parks Commission. He completed the Chef Apprenticeship program at Niagara College in 1983. He has attended the Culinary Institute of America for continuing education courses. Barry is the recipient of the Outstanding Achievement Award from the Ontario Government Ministry of Colleges and Universities.

For the past several years he has been chef at Queenston Heights Restaurant, owned by the Niagara Parks Commission. This excellent restaurant is situated on the Niagara Escarpment with a breathtaking view of the village of Queenston and the lower Niagara River.

Barry enjoys working in an area so rich in fresh produce and award winning wines and believes that Niagara chefs have a mandate to develop innovative menus which take advantage of these products.

A Taste of Portugal

DESOUSA WINE CELLARS

If you want a taste of Portugal, a visit to Desousa Wine Cellars is a must. The beautiful pink winery building with surrounding glorious flower beds, the crusty bread fresh from the bakery offered by one of the DeSousa family in the wine boutique, the 270-year old wine press display, as well as the full bodied wine tastings presented in clay bowls, all make you feel part of the Old World.

And the DeSousas know about that world. The antique wine press was built in 1820 in Portugal for the DeSousas who were grape growers on the island of St. Michael's in the Azores and sold their wines to wine merchants. Grape growing and winemaking have been passed down through four generations to John DeSousa Jr. who works with his father at the Vineland winery.

When the DeSousas came to Canada in 1961 they initially established a jewellery business before moving into the restaurant business in 1976 in Toronto. They opened a Portuguese restaurant, Lisbon By Night in which they now have a minority interest. The wine business, however, was always in John DeSousa's blood and he purchased vineyards in Niagara in 1979 which he replanted with French hybrid and vinifera. The winery was established in 1979 and three years later they opened the new building.

Unlike most of the Niagara wineries, 95 per cent of their production is red wine. The red and white wines are primarily full bodied, robust and dry because of their appeal to the Portuguese and Italian communities who buy about 85 per cent of the DeSousa production. They are excellent with spicy meat or pasta dishes. Aged in massive 990 gallon oak puncheons, these wines are put in 1.5 litre and 4 litre bottles because, as John DeSousa Jr. explains, the Portuguese and Italians like their wine that way. For those with slightly different tastes, DeSousa Wine Cellars also produces a premium Chardonnay, a Cabernet Franc and an

Icewine. They have also produced a unique product for Niagara, a 1986 Port from Marechal Foch grapes, which has been very popular and which they hope to duplicate again.

The Portuguese have always drank their wine from clay bowls, in part because they say the clay keeps the wine cooler in the summer and makes the wine smoother than in a glass.

The best way to find out is to visit DeSousa Wine Cellars where they will give you an opportunity to taste the wines in both along with a piece of wonderful crusty fresh bread.

Shrimp Casserole

24 shrimps
¼ cup (50 mL) butter
4 bay leaves
  juice of ½ lemon
½ cup (100 mL) dry white wine
1 bunch parsley

In a frying pan, melt ¼ cup (50 mL) of butter. Add juice of ½ lemon and pepper to taste. When this mixture is hot, add the shrimps and ½ cup (100 mL) of white wine. Let the shrimps cook for approximately 3 to 4 minutes, stirring constantly.

Remove from heat and serve immediately on a platter. Sprinkle with parsley.

Serves 4

Preparation time is about 15 minutes.

Shrimp Casserole
DeSousa 1992 Chardonnay

Porco Alentejana
DeSousa 1992 Marechal Foch

Curd Cheesecake

Above: *Porco Alentejana*
Opposite page: *Shrimp Casserole*

Porco Alentejana

2 lb (900 g) pork tenderloin
¼ cup (50 mL) vegetable oil
6 cloves of garlic
4 bay leaves
½ tsp (2.5 g) paprika
1 tbsp (20 g) diced coriander
24 clams garnished with pieces of
  pickles and black olives
2 cups (500 mL) dry white wine

Marinate pork tenderloin for 24 hours in casserole dish with cloves, bay leaves, paprika, coriander, wine and clams.

Pour ¼ cup of vegetable oil in a frying pan and, when very hot, add the pork tenderloin. Let it cook, stirring often, for 15 to 20 minutes. Add the well washed, diced coriander and ⅓ cup (75 mL) of dry white wine. Allow to cook for another 5 minutes, or until the wine evaporates. Serve immediately.

Serves 4

Preparation time, not including the 24 hours to marinate, is about 30 minutes.

Right: *John, John Jr. and Maria DeSousa*

Curd Cheesecake

¾ cup (100 g) flour
1½ tbsp (30 g) butter

Use enough water to blend these ingredients until there is a fine dough to cover a cake pan.

FOR FILLING
5 cups (500 g) curd cheese
3 eggs
a pinch of sugar
½ cup (50 g) flour
1 tsp (5 g) royal powder

For filling, blend all together, with the exception of the eggs. Then add 3 egg whites and beat until firm. Bake in oven at 300F (150°C) until golden brown.

Serves 4

Preparation time is approximately 1 hour.

CHEF GABRIEL DEFREITAS

Gabriel has been in the hotel and restaurant business for 29 years.

He trained at the Inn On The Park in Toronto, learning about the preparation of food from a number of well-known chefs who worked there over several years.

Always interested in Portuguese cuisine, he owned two Portuguese restaurants prior to his ownership of Lisbon By Night.

🐚 About the Wines 🐚

Gabriel explains that the crisp, clean VQA approved Chardonnay provides an excellent balance with the shrimp dish.

The robust, flavourful Marechal Foch matches very well with a white meat such as the marinated pork tenderloin.

DeSousa also offers an excellent 1986 Port wine that has been matured for eight years in oak.

A Summer Banquet in an Historical Setting

HENRY OF PELHAM ESTATE WINERY

Henry of Pelham isn't just another bench winery—it's an historical site. President Paul Speck, his brother, vineyard manager Matthew, and another brother Daniel, who is still in school, trace their heritage back to 1794 when the land on which the winery is located was part of a land grant given to their ancestors, Nicholas Smith and his family. Nicholas was a bugle boy for the famous Butler's Rangers and after the American Revolutionary War was one of the founders of the City of St. Catharines, Ontario.

One of Nicholas' sons, Henry, who became known as Henry of Pelham, built Henry Smith's tavern in 1842 which served as an inn and toll-gate for more than 100 years. The inn is now the Henry of Pelham Family Estate Winery. To enter the wine boutique, you must walk down the same stone steps as the visitors did to Henry Smith's tavern in the early 1800s. The same baker's oven that served those visitors is still present in the boutique.

The Smith family was one of the first to cultivate domestic grapes in the Niagara Region and a 75-year old vineyard still exists on the estate. Established in 1988, Henry of Pelham produces 15 varietal wines from their bench winery with most of the grapes originating from their 75 acre estate. They were one of the first estate wineries in Niagara dedicated to producing premium quality wines from 100 percent Ontario grown grapes.

The modern winery is equipped with state-of-the-art crusher, press, tanks and bottling line to meet the high standards of quality set by the Speck family. Old world winemaking matched with new world technology. Typical of the bench wineries, its wines display the distinctive character produced from the clay soil, the climate and the growing season along the ridge of the Niagara Escarpment. Among a number of excellent wines, winemaker Ron Giesbrecht who has significant experience in the Niagara wine industry, produces three Chardonnays including an award winning barrel-fermented and three Rieslings which are well worth tasting. All of the wines are produced to the Vintners Quality Alliance (VQA) standards.

For wine tasting in an historical setting or for a family picnic or barbeque visit Henry of Pelham. You'll be glad you did.

Duck Liver and Apple with Endives

- 3 large matsu apples
- 3 large shallots, peeled and sliced
- ½ lb (225g) fresh duck liver
- 1 bunch of Italian parsley
- 1½ tablespoons (30 mL) Calvados (apple brandy from France)
- ⅓ cup (75 mL) butter
- salt and black pepper
- 1 small head of frisée or curly endive
- olive oil

Slice 2 of the apples, unpeeled, into 20 very thin discs. Place a large frying pan over medium heat. Place the apple discs in the hot frying pan and caramelize on one side. Set aside.

Peel and core the remaining apple and cut into small cubes. Slice the shallots and roughly chop the parsley. Melt the butter in the frying pan and gently sauté the shallots and apples over medium heat. Add the liver, salt and black pepper and continue to saute for 2 minutes.

Stir in the Calvados and then invert the contents of the frying pan onto a baking tray. Refrigerate the liver mixture until well chilled.

Lay out 5 apple slices in an overlapping circle pattern on a large cloth napkin. Place some liver mixture into the center of the apples. Gather up the napkin all around the liver mixture so that the apple slices completely enclose the liver mixture in the shape of a ball. Repeat the process until there are 4 apple and liver balls. Then place them on a tray and into an oven at 250F (120°C) to warm.

Meanwhile, arrange frisee leaves or curly endive in a pleasing pattern around 4 plates. Sprinkle with olive oil, salt and pepper. After apple and liver mixture is thoroughly warm, or approximately 25 minutes, transfer one to each of the plates. Serve.

Serves 4

Preparation time is approximately 40 minutes.

Shrimp and Swiss Chard Roll in Fennel and Tomato Bouillon

FOR FENNEL AND TOMATO BOUILLON

1 bulb fennel

2 medium sized onions

1 leek

6 very ripe tomatoes

2 garlic bulbs

   zest of one orange

   pinch of saffron

1 celery stalk

½ nutmeg, grated

6 egg whites

   salt and black pepper

FOR SHRIMP AND SWISS CHARD ROLL

8 peeled, deveined, large fresh shrimp

½ lb (225 g) fresh scallops

2 egg yolks

1 tbsp (20 g) butter

2 tsp (10 mL) tarragon vinegar

¼ cup (50 mL) 35% whipping cream

   salt and pepper

3 large swiss chard leaves

Opposite page: *Duck Liver and Apple with Endives*
Above: *Shrimp and Swiss Chard Roll in Fennel and Tomato Bouillon*

To prepare fennel and tomato bouillon, place fennel, onions, leek, tomatoes, garlic, saffron, celery, nutmeg, and zest of orange in food processor and roughly dice. Transfer to a stainless steel pot and add egg whites, salt, and black pepper. Combine all ingredients well with a wooden spoon. Add 4½ cups (1 litre) of water and place over low heat stirring occasionally. After bouillon comes to a boil, cover and continue to simmer for 1 hour. Strain through a sieve.

To prepare shrimp and swiss chard roll, blanch swiss chard leaves in boiling water for 1 minute. Remove and lay them on cloths to dry. Make a paste of the scallops, using a food processor, then slowly add the egg yolks, salt and pepper, tarragon vinegar, whipping cream, and butter. Spread the scallop mixture on each blanched chard leaf

and add shrimp down the center of each. Roll each leaf with the mixture into a big "cigar", then poach them in water for 5 minutes until scallop paste is set. Slice rounds of chard roll and place in wide-brimmed soup bowls. Pour piping hot tomato fennel bouillon over the chard rolls and serve immediately.

Serves 4

Preparation time is approximately 1½ hours.

Top: *Roasted Beef Tenderloin with Small Vegetables and Fresh Horseradish*

Right: *Chocolate and Vanilla Cones with Black Currant and Blood Orange*

Roasted Beef Tenderloin with Small Vegetables and Fresh Horseradish

1½ lb (750 g) beef tenderloin in one piece, seasoned with salt, pepper and garlic.

1 squash

1 piece of fresh horseradish

8 small carrots

8 small potatoes

8 small turnips

1 leek, cleaned

2 cups (500 mL) beef bouillon

   sprigs of fresh parsley

Roast squash, scoop out the flesh and purée in food processor. Peel and cook the carrots and turnip, and scrub and cook the potatoes. Wash the leek and slice into diamond shapes. Roast the beef tenderloin at 375F (190°C) for approximately 15 minutes, to reach medium. Remove from oven and allow to sit. Garnish each plate with the variety of vegetables, then heat the beef bouillon and pour onto each plate. Slice the beef tenderloin and place on plates. Grate fresh horseradish over each dish. Serve immediately.

Serves 4

Preparation time is about 45 minutes.

Chocolate and Vanilla Cones with Black Currant and Blood Orange

½ cup (60 g) pastry flour

¼ cup (60 g) butter

¼ cup (60 g) liquid egg white

¼ cup (60 g) sugar

   one vanilla bean, split lengthwise and scooped out

   black currants

   sugar

4 blood oranges

   vanilla ice cream, good quality

   chocolate ice cream, good quality

To prepare cones, cream the butter and sugar together. Alternate the egg white, pastry flour and the vanilla bean. Drop tablespoon sized dollops of batter onto greased cookie sheets. Spread the dollops into oval shaped thins and bake at 400F (205°C) until golden around edges. Remove and roll while still hot into 8 cone shapes.

Cook currants with half their weight in sugar for 10 minutes. Let cool.

Squeeze 2 blood oranges for juice and then reduce with ⅓ cup (75 mL) of sugar to a syrup. Remove all the skin, pith, and section 2 blood oranges.

Place a small scoop of vanilla ice cream into 4 cones and place on the plates. Do the same with the chocolate ice cream. Warm the black currant compote and place on one side of each plate. Place the blood orange sections with blood orange glaze on the other.

Serves 4

Preparation time is approximately 1 hour.

Above *Winemaker Ron Giesbrecht and Paul and Matthew Speck.*

❧ About the Wines ❧

Chef Jamie Kennedy chose the Riesling with the duck liver for its fruity character which lends itself well to the apple and liver combination of the dish.

In choosing the Chardonnay with the shrimp and swiss chard roll, he explains: "The neutrality of the dish allows the complexity of this well structured Chardonnay to show itself brilliantly."

He picked the Baco Noir as a match with the beef tenderloin because it is an excellent food wine, particularly well suited to red meats such as beef or lamb.

CHEF JAMIE KENNEDY

Jamie is widely recognized as one of Canada's outstanding chefs. Trained in Toronto at the former Windsor Arms Hotel, he also spent some time in Europe as an apprentice. He has represented Canada at an international food competition in France and has written a cookbook which was published in 1985.

For the past nine years, Jamie has been chef and partner at the popular and widely acclaimed Palmerston Restaurant in Toronto. He has also worked as the chef at The Founders' Club in Toronto's SkyDome, home of baseball's world champion Blue Jays.

A Charming Escarpment Winery

HERNDER ESTATE WINES

Hernder is the newest of the small bench wineries, located in a 127-year old Victorian stone barn on the beautiful Escarpment.

Originally a barn used for raising cattle, it has been completely renovated into a modern, state-of-the-art winery and juice processing facility.

Although the winery is new, the Hernder family is not new to the grape business. Since 1939, the Hernders have been growing grapes for the juice and wine industries. Fred Hernder sold supplies for the home wine market for years and operated a juice plant called The Wine Barn on his 250 acre property.

With several wineries in the area, there were many visitors to Hernder's Barn who thought they were operating a winery and wanted tastings and a tour. Fred Hernder says, "One thing led to another and we decided it made sense for us to open a winery." Hernder Estate Wines opened their retail store in 1992.

All members of the Hernder family work in the wine business, including Fred's wife, Ricki-Lynn, his daughter Angel, and son, Chris. Joining Hernder in 1992 as winemaker was Ray Cornell, who has 12 years experience in the Niagara wine business, and who has won several wine awards at international competitions.

Hernder's wines are all VQA approved and include Vidal Dry and Semi-Dry, Riesling, Chardonnay, and Cabernet Franc.

Tastings are available at the winery boutique, and tours are also available at certain times.

Left: *A selection of wines in the boutique*
Centre: *Winemaker Ray Cornell*
Below: *Chris, Anjel and Fred Hernder*

Trisha Romance

Trisha is one of Canada's most popular and successful artists. She got off to an early start. The drive to capture her immediate surroundings and find inspiration in everyday events of life can be traced to when she was only five years old.

Today, the popularity of her paintings is growing faster than her ability to supply the demand. Fortunately, since 1980 limited edition reproductions from the originals have allowed collectors to enjoy her artwork.

Trisha was born in Western New York and moved to Canada in 1969 to attend Sheridan College in Oakville, Ontario where she received a degree in design and illustra-

tion. She now lives in Niagara-On-The-Lake with her husband, Gary, and their three children, Nathan,

Tanya and Whitney, who have become the loving focus of her many paintings in watercolour. The recently published book, *The World of Trisha Romance*, is a tribute to her lifetime of work.

"I enjoy cooking tremendously when I have the sweet luxury of time, good friends, and family to share it with. Since the essence of my work is often a vignette of motherhood, kitchen scenes are a vital part of everyday life with my family."

This Mushroom Burgundy recipe was introduced to Trisha 14 years ago by her sister, Jeanne, now living in Alaska. "Every time it's resurrected, it brings back fond memories of our time shared together."

About the Wines

Two wines that match well with the Mushroom Burgundy are Marynissen Estates Cabernet Sauvignon and Stonechurch Vineyards Cabernet Franc.

Mushroom Burgundy

4 lbs (about 3 cups — 750 g) fresh
   mushrooms

4 cloves garlic

3 medium bell peppers, 1 red, 1
   yellow, 1 green

2 spanish onions

½ cup (115 g) butter

¾ cup (175 g) chopped watercress

⅓ cup (75 g) Dijon mustard

⅓ cup (75 mL) Worcestershire sauce

½ cup (85 g) brown sugar

3 to 4 cups (700–900 mL) full
   bodied dry red wine
   fresh ground black pepper
   salt

Wash and de-stem the mushrooms and, unless quite small, cut in half. Wash and seed peppers and cut in approximately 1 inch squares. Peel and chop onion and garlic. Melt butter in deep dish frying pan and sauté onion and garlic until transparent.

To prepare sauce, mix together mustard, sugar and Worcestershire sauce to a smooth paste. Add 3 cups (700 mL) of wine and season with salt and pepper. Stir well.

When onion is clear, add all but 1 cup (250 g) of mushroom caps and peppers and sauté. As mushrooms begin to brown and shrink, add wine sauce. Simmer over medium heat for 45 minutes or until sauce is reduced and thick. During the last 15 minutes of simmering add the last cup of mushrooms and remaining wine as needed. Just before serving mix in watercress. Mushrooms and peppers will be dark, but will have incredible flavour and aroma.

Serve over white rice.

Serves 4 to 6

Preparation time is approximately 1 hour.

A Delectable Choice for Entertaining

HILLEBRAND ESTATES WINERY

As one of Canada's biggest wineries, Hillebrand is a major force in the wine industry. It is very proud of its Canadian identity which it displays in such innovative ways as producing an annual series of Limited Edition labels based on the Group of Seven paintings.

The winery began operating in Niagara-On-The-Lake in 1982. Today, it sells its wine through more than 50 of its own retail stores across the country and other distribution channels. Hillebrand has 35 acres—10 of which are used for experimentation—and contracts with 40 winegrowers in the Niagara Region. The winery, which has an excellent reputation built on quality, is the largest seller of VQA wines in

Canada. It also is well known internationally selling about five percent of its production in the international market. George Sorensen, president of Hillebrand, says that 50 per cent of its production will soon be varietal wines. The winery is constantly adding new products created by its two winemakers, Jean-Laurent Groux and Laurent Dal'Zovo. Jean-Laurent was trained in Bordeaux and Germany and Laurent in Montpelier and California.

They produced the first sparkling wine in Canada made by the *methode champenoise* which uses 85 per cent Chardonnay and 15 per cent Pinot Noir grapes. The bottles are painstakingly turned by hand and must sit 15 months to develop complexity. The result is a fine, pale gold bubbly. Hillebrand's flagship wines are the Trius Collection which include three excellent Chardonnays from vineyards in different areas of Niagara, a Riesling, and a red wine made from a blend of Cabernet Sauvignon, Merlot and Cabernet Franc.

Hillebrand puts a great deal of emphasis on the combination of food and wine and cross-merchandises them in a number of fine food retail stores. As part of their effort to make the wines consumer-friendly, they have introduced a "Harvest Classics Series" which matches foods with particular wines printed on the back labels of the bottles. The Harvest Classics Series wines were produced to offer quality at economical prices and include a Muscat Reserve, Gewurztraminer, Pinot Gris, Gamay Noir, Riesling and a Chardonnay. Depending on the varietal, small amounts of the wine are aged in oak and then blended back into the whole so that the oak's presence is a nuance or complexity and does not dominate the wine.

One of the great events in the Niagara Region is the Jazz Festival held each year at Hillebrand. Attracting about 3,000 people, this happening is worthwhile attending and provides a good opportunity to taste Hillebrand wines while enjoying the food and music. Hillebrand provides tours of its excellent facilities on a regular basis.

❧ MENU ❧

Pepper Seared Blue Fin Tuna With Soy Butter Sauce
Hillebrand 1992 Riesling

Mediterranean Summers Night Terrine
Hillebrand Mounier Brut

Grilled Beef Tenderloin With Roasted Potatoes,
Olive Oil And Balsamic Vinegar
Hillebrand Trius Red

Pepper Seared Blue Fin Tuna with Soy Butter Sauce

Allow ¼ lb (115 g) of tuna per person

      cracked black peppercorn
  2 shallots, thinly sliced
  1 cup (250 mL) white wine
1½ tbsp (30 mL) rice wine vinegar
  ¼ cup (50 mL) cream
1½ cups (350 g) butter
      soy sauce
      lime juice
      salt
      fresh coriander leaves
      diced tomato

Press the tuna into the pepper to coat the tuna on one side.

Place the shallots in a thick-bottomed pan and cook in a little butter until soft. Add the wine vinegar, reduce until almost dry, then add the cream and whisk in the butter. Season with soy sauce, lime juice, tomato and coriander.

Pan-sear the tuna until medium rare and serve with the sauce.

Preparation time is about 30 minutes.

Opposite page: *Pepper Seared Blue Fin Tuna With Soy Butter Sauce*

Above:: *Mediterranean Summers Night Terrine*

Mediterranean Summers Night Terrine

  2 1 lb (500 g) lobsters, cooked, shelled out and cut into large cubes
  ½ lb (200 g) American red snapper filet, cut into large cubes
  ½ lb (200 g) halibut filet, cut into large cubes
  ½ lb (200 g) Black Sea bass, cut into large cubes
  ½lb (200 g) lotte fish, cut into large cubes (other fish can be substituted)
  3 stalks celery, sliced neatly
  1 large fennel bulb, sliced neatly
3½ cups (750 mL) clear fish stock large pinch saffron threads
  6 to 8 gelatin leaves
  1 small bunch chives, chopped
  ¼ bunch parsley, chopped
  1 small bunch basil, chopped salt and pepper to taste pinch cayenne pepper

Grilled Beef Tenderloin with Roasted Vegetables, Olive Oil and Balsamic Vinegar

4 ½ lb (200 g) portions of beef tenderloin
2 large globe artichokes
8 fingerling potatoes, cooked and peeled (can be obtained at organic markets, or other potatoes can be used)
1 small red pepper, roasted, peeled and cut into large cubes
1 small yellow pepper, roasted, peeled and cut into large cubes
8 pearl onions, peeled
8 large shitake mushrooms, quartered
2 lemons
4 sprigs fresh thyme
1 large clove garlic, finely chopped
  handful of French green beans, blanched and refreshed
4 sprigs parsley, leaves only, shredded
  salt and pepper
  balsamic vinegar
  extra virgin olive oil and pure olive oil

Bring the fish stock to a simmer, add the fennel and celery, and cook until tender. Remove and leave to cool. Add the fish, except the lobster, to the stock and cook until just done. Lift out and leave to cool.

Strain the cooking liquid through a coffee filter into a clean bowl. Add the saffron and allow to infuse for approximately 10 minutes. Soak the gelatin leaves in cold water until soft, and dissolve in saffron liquid. Test a small amount of liquid on a cold plate and place in refrigerator. It should set firm, but not rubbery.

Season the fish, lobster and veg-etables with salt, pepper and cayenne. Sprinkle with the chopped herbs. Pour a layer of liquid, about ¼ inch (5 mm) thick, into the terrine. Place in the refrigerator to set.

Start building up layers of fish and vegetables in the terrine, then pour in the liquid to cover all. Cover with a plastic wrap and leave overnight in the refrigerator so that the flavours can develop. Slice with a hot knife and serve with a salad or vegetables in vinaigrette.

Serves 4

Preparation time is about 1 hour, but must be prepared the day before.

Trim the artichokes down to the heart. Rub with the lemon to prevent dis-colouration. Cut each heart into 8 seg-ments and remove the choke. Squeeze the remaining lemon over them.

Heat the pure olive oil in a large pan and add the pearl onions, arti-chokes, shitake mushrooms, potatoes

says chef Keith Froggett. "The wine must be well chilled and the tuna kept on the rare side to prevent it from becoming dry.

"Mounier Brut has a complex aroma and a lively crispness which complement the subtle flavours and textures of the fish terrine. The terrine should be served at room temperature and the wine very chilled.

and thyme. Toss together and roast in a moderately hot oven until slightly coloured and tender. Add the garlic, peppers, beans, parsley, a little extra virgin olive oil, and salt and pepper.

Bring the meat to room temperature, then rub with olive oil, salt and pepper, and grill until medium rare, approximately 4 or 5 minutes per side over a hot grill. Leave for 2 or 3 minutes in a warm place. Arrange the vegetables on a platter. Slice the meat in half and place on top of the vegetables. Drizzle with more extra virgin olive oil and then balsamic vinegar.

Serves 4

Preparation time is approximately 50 minutes.

🗟 About the Wines 🗟

"The Hillebrand Riesling has crisp, fruity flavours balanced with a little sweetness, which act as a nice foil for the peppery tuna and piquant sauce,"

"Trius Red is a perfect accompaniment to the grilled beef tenderloin. The wine possesses rich aroma and a little spiciness which stand up well with the rich flavour of the grilled meat and the slightly sweet taste of the roasted vegetables and balsamic vinegar. Be sure to let the meat relax for two or three minutes after cooking and before slicing as this will ensure an even distribution of juice inside the meat. When pouring the wine, let it splash into the glass so as to aerate it and enhance the flavours and bouquet."

CHEF KEITH FROGGETT

Keith received his training as a chef in England, the last 18 months of which was spent at Claridges Hotel in London. He moved to Canada in 1979 and worked at the Sutton Place Hotel in Toronto. From there he went to the Four Seasons Inn on the Park in Toronto, and from there to the former Fenton's restaurant.

Keith has been working at Scaramouche, one of Toronto's finest restaurants, since 1983 and has been Chef since 1986. He notes that Ontario wines have made "leaps and bounds" over the past few years. He particularly likes to have an Ontario Riesling as an aperitif, and also likes some of the other white and red wines with dinner.

A Formal Dinner in the Loft

INNISKILLIN

I t's been 20 years since Donald Ziraldo and Karl Kaiser teamed up to establish the first boutique winery in the Province of Ontario. They have come a long way since then.

Today Inniskillin is renowned internationally as a world class boutique winery and presents an image of quality, sophistication and class as a leader in the industry. It's a remarkable progression considering the many obstacles faced by Donald and Karl when they first began operating. After they were granted the first winery license in Ontario since 1929, wine experts told them that European vinifera varieties were not commercially viable in Canada. They had to rise above the poor image of the Canadian wine industry in the 1970's, and did that by providing quality products and a matching image. Only five years ago the wine critics said that fine red wines could not be produced in the Niagara Region. Inniskillin and other boutique wineries proved them wrong, supporting Karl's contention that Niagara's growing season mirrors Burgundy.

Although Donald and Karl are different in may respects, their mutual love of wine is a very strong bond. Donald grew up watching his father grow grapes for the Canadian wine industry and make wine for the family. As a university student studying horticulture he wrote about growth curves in grape production. Today he is still happiest when riding his tractor in the vineyards. Karl's old world knowledge and love of wines comes from his years spent at a private school in Austria run by Cisterian monks where he studied their ties to Burgundian viticulture and sampled vintages with the monks.

Their partnership has worked well. While Donald handles the business and marketing aspects of the company and acts as an ambassador for the industry, Karl is the winemaker and restless experimenter looking to develop new products. Innis-killin grows approximately 30 per cent of its own grapes on its 45 acre Brae Burn Estate and works with a select group of Ontario grape growers. The owner of the farm where the winery began operations, Colonel Cooper, was granted Crown land along the Niagara River and named it after the Irish Regiment, the Inniskilling Fusiliers. Karl believes that Chardonnay and Pinot Noir are the wines of the future because of the cool climatic conditions in Niagara. He has been producing Chardonnays since 1977, broadening his selections to include a Chardonnay Reserve and a signature series of Chardonnays from specific vineyards—Seeger, Montague, Schuele, and Klose.

One of Donald's greatest contributions to the wine industry has been as chairman and founder of the VQA, Vintner's Quality Alliance, a system showing appelation of origin and providing standards to ensure quality products for consumers. The VQA has played a vital role in giving the

❦ MENU ❧

*Prawn and Pancetta Skewers with
Chive and Watercress Sauces*
*Inniskillin 1992 Chardonnay
Reserve*

*Pepper Crusted Pork Tenderloin
with Rosemary Tomato Coulis
and Garlic Confit*
Inniskillin 1992 Pinot Noir Reserve

*Champagne Mousse Torte
with Orange Sauce*
*Inniskillin L'Allemand Champagne
or Inniskillin Icewine*

Ontario wine industry credibility in the international wine market.

Visiting Inniskillin is a total wine experience. Apart from its charm and beautiful location, the self guided tour conceived by Donold Ziraldo and Deborah Pratt, who has been with Inniskillin almost since the beginning and has played a vital role in the development of its image as Director of Public Relations, provides one of the most complete tour programs in North America. The tour features 20 stations depicting and explaining every phase of grape growing and winemaking from the vineyard to the tasting room. An art gallery featuring Canadian artists in the

boutique loft adds to the ambience.

Donald Ziraldo was once quoted as saying: "If you're going to be an actor, you have to make it in Hollywood. If you're going to be a winemaker you have to make it in Paris." Inniskillin has had selected representation in Paris through Le Repaire de Bacchus. Their most significant recognition to date came at the world's foremost wine show, Vin Expo in Bordeaux, in 1991. Among 4100 international competitors, Inniskillin's 1989 Icewine was awarded the Grand Prix D'Honneur—the equivalent of an Olympic Gold Medal in the international wine business which awakened the international

wine world to the quality of Niagara wines. A visit to the Niagara Wine Region is not complete without a visit to Inniskillin.

Prawn and Pancetta Skewers with Chive and Watercress Sauces

20 large prawns, peeled and deveined
8 slices pancetta cut into ⅜th inch (1 cm) strips
1 tbsp butter
4 medium size metal skewers

CHIVE SAUCE:
2 shallots minced
¾ cup (200 ml) dry white wine

¾ cup (200 ml) fish stock
½ cup (125 ml) cream
1 tbsp fresh chives finely chopped
¾ cup (175g cup) cold butter
   salt, pepper

WATERCRESS SAUCE:
1 bunch watercress, cleaned and washed
½ cup (125 ml) dry white wine
1 cup (250 ml) fish stock
1 shallot, minced
1 clove garlic, minced
½ cup (125 ml) cream
   salt, pepper

Wrap each prawn with a slice of pancetta and thread 5 wrapped prawns onto each skewer.

Opposite page, top left: *Donald Ziraldo and Karl Kaiser (left)*
Opposite page, bottom right: *Deborah Pratt*
Above: *Prawn and Pancetta Skewers*

CHIVE SAUCE
Place shallots and wine in a small pan. Cook to a glaze. Add stock and continue simmering until 2 tbsp. remain. Add cream, continue simmering for five more minutes. Strain through a sieve. Add chives, lower heat to minimum and whisk in butter piece by piece. Take off heat, adjust seasoning and place in hot waterbath to keep warm.

WATERCRESS SAUCE
Blanch watercress for 10 minutes in salted water. Drain and refresh with cold water. Purée in food processor and set aside. Simmer wine, stock, shallots and garlic in a small saucepan for about five minutes. Add puréed watercress and strain through a sieve. Add cream and simmer for a few more minutes. Season with salt and pepper, and keep warm in hot waterbath.

Heat 1 tbsp. of butter in a medium size frying pan and fry the skewers on both sides until pancetta is crisp and prawns are cooked, or about 2 minutes each side. Place one skewer on each serving plate with 1 tbsp. of sauce on either side.

Serves 4

Preparation time is approximately 40 minutes.

Pepper Crusted Pork Tenderloin with Rosemary Tomato Coulis and Garlic Confit

½ lb (700g) pork tenderloin, whole
2 tbsp crushed black peppercorns
  salt
2 tbsp of oil
½ cup (125 ml) of red wine
4 ripe tomatoes, peeled, seeded and chopped
1 tbsp of tomato concentrate
5 sprigs of fresh rosemary

1 cup (250 ml) of chicken or beef stock
¾ cup (200 ml) of cream
2 tbsp of cold butter, cut into small pieces
  salt
  freshly ground pepper

GARLIC CONFIT
10 garlic cloves, unpeeled
2 tbsp of olive oil
1 sprig of fresh thyme
  salt
  pepper

Preheat oven to 450F (230°C). In a skillet just large enough to hold the pork tenderloin, heat oil over high heat. Press peppercorns onto all sides of pork, sprinkle with salt and brown well on all sides. Take skillet off heat, remove pork, wrap tightly in aluminum foil and transfer to preheated oven for 15 to 20 minutes.

Meanwhile, pour out excess grease from skillet and de-glaze with wine. Add tomatoes, tomato concentrate, rosemary, and garlic. Cook, stirring for a few minutes. Add stock and simmer for 2 to 3 minutes. Lower heat, whisk in butter, season with salt and pepper. Keep warm.

Take pork tenderloin out of oven, unwrap, pour excess juices into sauce. Slice tenderloin into medallions and serve with tomato rosemary sauce and garlic confit.

CONFIT
Preheat oven to 200F (100°C). In a small ovenproof dish pour in oil, place garlic cloves on top, coat well with oil, add sprig of thyme, cover with aluminium foil and bake for 1 hour. Take dish out of oven, let cool slightly and squeeze garlic out of skin. Mash with fork and season to taste with salt and pepper.

Serves 4.

Preparation time is about 1 hour.

Left: *Pepper Crusted Pork Tenderloin*
Opposite page: *Champagne Mousse Torte*

Champagne Mousse Torte with Orange Sauce

1 cup (250 mL) of Inniskillin
  L'Allemand Champagne
4 eggs
4 tbsp (50g) sugar
1 tbsp (20g) sugar
1 vanilla bean, split lengthwise
4 gelatin leaves
1 cup (250 mL) of whipping cream
2 tbsp (30 mL) of Grand Marnier

SPONGE CAKE LAYERS

6 eggs, room temperature
1 cup (200g) of sugar
¾ cup (150g) of flour
⅓ cup (45g) of unsweetened cacao
3 tbsp (45g) of melted butter

ORANGE SAUCE

1 cup (200g) of sugar
juice from 1 lemon
3 cups (750 mL) of orange juice

SPONGE LAYERS

Preheat oven to 375F (190°C). Generously butter 2 baking sheets and sprinkle lightly with flour. Using an electric mixer, beat eggs with sugar on a low speed for 5 minutes. Increase speed to medium, beat for another 5 minutes, repeat at high speed. Turn mixer off, sift flour and cacao together and gently fold in egg mixture. Now fold in melted butter. Spread a thin layer of batter onto each baking sheet and bake for 8 to 10 minutes or until set. Take sponge cakes out of oven, unmold and let cool.

MOUSSE

In a medium bowl, whisk egg yolks with ¼ cup (50g) of sugar. Soften gelatin leaves in cold water. Aside, bring champagne and vanilla to boil, quickly whisk champagne into egg mixture and put back on low heat. Continue whisking until mixture thickens. Do not let boil. Immediately take off heat, squeeze excess water out of gelatin leaves, add them to hot mixture and whisk until they dissolve. Let cool. Beat cream until soft peaks form. Aside, beat egg whites until stiff, add ⅛ cup (20g) of sugar and continue beating for 1 more minute. Gently combine champagne mixture with cream and egg whites. Chill until mousse starts to thicken and can be spread without running.

Cut each sponge layer into 2. Place a rectangle of sponge cake on a platter. Moisten a pastry brush with Grand Marnier. Spoon ¼ of mousse evenly on top, cover with another sponge layer, moisten with Grand Marnier, spoon another ¼ of mousse on top and continue layers complete. Once last layer of mousse is spread, refrigerate torte until set, (2 to 3 hours). Trim sides of torte before serving. Serve with orange sauce.

ORANGE SAUCE

In a saucepan, melt sugar and lemon juice over high heat until it turns a deep caramel colour. Take off heat, add orange juice a little bit at a time. Stand back, as the caramel may bubble vigorously. Stir well and let cool.

🌿 **About the Wines** 🌿

The 1992 Chardonnay Reserve was chosen by Izabela because the rich creaminess of this heavier Chardonnay matches well with the sweetness of the prawns and the touch of acidity in the wine cuts through and offsets the buttery tastes of the watercress and chive sauces.

The 1992 Pinot Noir Reserve is a delicate wine. The fresh, fruitiness of the wine works well with, not overpowering, the different flavours of the meat, tomatoes and garlic. The ripe cherry and berry fruit with chocolate overtones marry beautifully with the variety of herbs in this entrée.

CHEF IZABELA KALABIS

A Niagara-On-The-Lake native, Izabela Kalabis brings haute cuisine to the tasting of this winery's fine wines. Her love of cooking was inspired by her first trip to the Loire Valley where she had planned to learn French as a tutor. She studied at La Varenne Cooking School in Paris and apprenticed at a number of reputable Parisian restaurants. Izabela was the author of the Wine and Food Adventure Card Series, pairing specific wines with specific foods. She also studied wine at L'Académie du Vin run by Stephen Sperrier. After further training, she worked for a while in France as a private chef and then returned to Canada, where she has since prepared many wonderful dishes for receptions, luncheons and formal dinners in Inniskillin's Champagne Loft, specializing in Canadian cuisine. Her talents inspired Inniskillin to schedule a number of loft dinners throughout the year which provide a showcase for her culinary expertise and for Inniskillin's wide range of wines.

A Summer Sunday Brunch

KITTLING RIDGE ESTATES

Behind Kittling Ridge the Escarpment rises very sharply. Each spring the sun-warmed air creates thermals attracting hawks and thousands of other migratory birds soaring effortlessly or "kittling" on the circling updrafts. It is the same ridge that creates the superb growing conditions for the grapes used in this winery's products.

Kittling Ridge Estates is a combined winery and distillery which provides some unique and excellent products. John Hall, one of the principal owners and president and CEO, has spent more than 25 years working to cultivate Ontario wine to world standards. John began his experience in the industry as a winemaker. As chairman of the Wine Council of Ontario in 1990, he spearheaded a successful advertising campaign advising consumers "We're Ready When You Are".

He has now embarked on generating further enhancements and innovative products for the industry through Kittling Ridge. For example, he

has developed an Icewine & Brandy, the only product of its kind in the world. It's a delicious blend of Vidal icewine and seven-year-old brandy to be enjoyed as an aperitif, or after dinner with cheese or fruit. The Icewine & Eau de Vie is also very popular.

Many of Kittling Ridge's spirit products, which bear the KR Distillery name, are produced from the flavourful peaches, cherries, plums, apples, pears, and grapes for which Niagara is so well known. These products range from traditional and fruit brandies aged in small oak barrels for as long as 10 years, to smooth whisky, vodka, rum and flavored liqueurs.

Kittling Ridge Estate table wines are produced from premium vinifera grape varieties including Sauvignon, Chardonnay, Riesling and Cabernet.

The winery provides tours of the distillery and winery and has a boutique wine shop which features their artwork, gifts and some of their products at a tasting bar.

Cherry Chèvre Spread

For brunch appetizer, put on toasted points of raisin bread or on small wedges of split toasted English muffins. Cherry chèvre spread makes a wonderful breakfast on its own, served on fresh baked scones.

- 1 cup (250 g) pitted sour cherries, canned in light syrup, well drained
- ½ cup (100 mL) Cabernet Sauvignon
- 2 tbsp (40 g) sugar
- 8 oz (250 g) Chèvre, plain flavour (goat cheese)
- 2 tbsp (40 g) unsalted butter, softened
- ¼ cup (55g) walnuts, freshly cracked, toasted and coarsely chopped

In small saucepan, combine cherries, wine and sugar.

On high heat, bring to a boil. Immediately lower to medium high heat and simmer, uncovered, until liquid is almost totally reduced, or for 15 to 17 minutes. Purée in blender and chill. In small mixing bowl, cream together the Chèvre and butter. Beat in the chilled cherry purée. Gently fold in the walnuts. Put into a crock and refrigerate until ready to serve. Makes 1½ cups (350 g).

Serves 8 to 10

Allow 1 hour for preparation, including time to chill the spread.

🎜 MENU 🎜

Cherry Chèvre Spread on assorted toast triangles
Kittling Ridge Cabernet Sauvignon

Strawberry Soup
Avocado, Orange and Pecan Salad with Honey Lime Dressing
Tomato-Spinach Spiral Bread
Mandarin Fettucini
Kittling Ridge Sauvignon Blanc

Iced Grapes
Chocolate Truffle Assortment
Kittling Ridge Icewine & Brandy

Strawberry Soup

1 pint (575 g) fresh strawberries
½ cup (100 mL) honey
½ cup (100 mL) light sour cream
1½ cups (350 mL) cold water
1 cup (250 mL) Cabernet
   Sauvignon

Place all ingredients in blender and liquefy. There will be tiny seeds visible, but straining is not necessary. Chill. Stir well before serving. Serve in wine glasses and garnish each with a fresh sprig of mint.

Serves 6 to 8

Preparation time is 15 minutes, plus chilling time.

Above: *Strawberry Soup*
Right: *Kittling Ridge Winemaker John Hall*

Avocado, Orange, Pecan Salad

6 cups (1.3 kg) assorted salad greens: Boston lettuce, radicchio, and curly endive
3 small navel oranges, peeled and sectioned
3 medium avocados, peeled and sliced
¾ cup (175 mL) mayonnaise
¼ cup (50 mL) honey
¼ cup (50 mL) fresh lime juice
3 tsp (15 g) rind of fresh limes, grated
½ cup (75 g) chopped pecans
optional: 3 peeled, sliced kiwi fruit and 6 whole strawberries for garnish

On six individual serving plates, place one cup of assorted greens. Arrange orange and avocado sections alternately in a circle on the greens. If using the

9 cups (1 kg) all purpose flour
5.5 oz (150 g) can tomato paste
1 egg white, mixed with 1 tbsp (20 mL) water

In a large measuring cup or small bowl, combine water and yeast. Let stand for three minutes to dissolve yeast. Stir in melted butter and salt.

Drain spinach in a strainer or sieve. With your hands, squeeze into a ball to extract all moisture. Place spinach in a food processor, and ¾ cup (175 g) of the yeast mixture. Cover and process until well mixed. Add ⅛ to one cup (55-115 g) flour until dough forms a stiff ball. Leave in food processor. Pour ¾ cup (175 g) of yeast mixture into a measuring bowl. Stir in tomato paste until well mixed. Stir in two cups of the flour until a stiff dough forms. Leave dough in bowl.

Pour remaining 1⅛ cups (350 g) of yeast mixture into a large bowl. Stir in three cups (340 g) of the flour until a stiff dough forms. Turn dough out onto a well floured surface and knead for five to 10 minutes, using only as much of the remaining flour as needed to keep it from sticking, about ¾ cup (80 g). Wash bowl and dry well. Oil the bowl and place dough in bowl. Turn dough to bring greased side up. Cover and let rise for 1½ hours.

Meanwhile, turn the spinach dough out onto well-floured surface and knead for five to 10 minutes, using only as much of the remaining flour as needed to keep it from sticking, about

kiwi fruit slices, add them in an alternating pattern. Stir together the mayonnaise, honey, lime juice and rind. This can be done ahead, to blend flavours. Spoon over the fruit slices, making a ring through the center of the fruit arrangement. Sprinkle on pecans and garnish with the whole strawberry. Do not hull the berry.

Serves 6

Preparation time is about 30 minutes.

Above: *Copper still used in distilling Kittling Ridge Icewine and Brandy*
Opposite: *Clockwise from bottom: Mandarin Fettucine, Avocado, Orange & Pecan Salad; Tomato-Spinach Spiral Bread*

Tomato-Spinach Spiral Bread

This recipe makes two huge loaves, so you may want to halve them to make four smaller loaves. The smaller loaf is a nice size for serving six people.

3 cups (700 mL) warm water, 110–115F (43–46°C)
2 packages active dry yeast
¼ cup (55 g) butter, melted
1 tbsp (20 g) salt
1 10 oz (285 g) pkg frozen chopped spinach (thawed)

⅛ cup (55 g). Place in greased medium bowl. Turn to bring greased side up. Cover and let rise for1½ hours.

Punch all doughs down and divide each into halves. Roll one half of the plain dough into a 9 inch (22.5 cm) square. Roll spinach and tomato doughs to the same size squares. Do not use too much flour while rolling, or doughs will not stick together. Place spinach layer on top of plain layer then top with tomato layer.

Roll the stack of dough into a 10 x 12 inch (25 x 30 cm) rectangle. Starting from the 12-inch edge, tightly roll dough jelly-roll style. At this point, cut each roll in half with a very sharp knife. This forms two loaves. Pinch seam to seal. With sides of hands, press ends of roll to seal taper slightly. Place loaf, seam side down, diagonally across a greased cookie sheet. Cover with a towel. Let rise in a warm place until doubled, or about 30 minutes.

Heat oven to 400F (205°C). Place a shallow pan of boiling water on bottom of oven. This will help to create steam for crispy crust. Brush egg white mixture on loaves. Slash center of the top of each loaf in a diamond pattern about ⅛ inch (0.3 cm) deep. Bake for 20 minutes. Switch cookie sheets between upper and lower oven racks so both loaves brown evenly. Brush again and bake for 25 minutes longer or until loaves sound hollow when lightly tapped with fingers. Remove to cool on wire racks. Store in plastic bags.

Mandarin Fettucini

1 lb (454 g) fettucini, fresh or dry
2 tsp (10 g) butter
1½ cups (350 mL) whipping cream, 35%
⅓ cup (75 mL) Sauvignon Blanc
2 egg yolks
½ cup (25 g) freshly grated Reggiano Parmesan cheese
½ lb (250 g) cooked, boneless, skinless, chicken breasts, cut into slivers
½ cup (75 g) sliced water chestnuts
9 oz (284 mL) canned mandarin oranges, well drained. Reserve 6 segments for garnish.
1 lemon, rind finely grated
¼ tsp (1 g) nutmeg, finely grated
¼ tsp (1 g) white pepper
   salt, to taste

Whisk together cream, egg yolks, white wine, and parmesan cheese. Add pasta to large pot of boiling, salted water. Cook until *al dente*.

In a very large skillet, melt butter. Drain the pasta and add it to the skillet. Sauté very lightly.

On medium heat, add the cream mixture and chicken slivers, water chestnuts, lemon rind, nutmeg, salt and pepper. Cook mixture, stirring and tossing until cream is reduced to desired consistency, slightly thickened. Do not boil or sauce will curdle. Add the mandarin oranges and gently toss, so as not to break the segments, just until they are heated through. Pour on to warmed serving platter and garnish. Serve immediately.

To garnish, sprinkle top with extra Reggiano Parmesan. Fan three of the reserved mandarin orange segments on either side of the platter. Intersperse with thin lemon slice twists.

Serves 4 to 6

Preparation time is about 30 minutes.

Iced Grapes

1   bunch red or green seedless grapes

Place the washed and dried grapes in the freezer overnight. When ready to serve, place on a glass or silver serving dish and immediately take to the table. The grapes frost beautifully when they come in contact with room temperature air. Enjoy the grapes when they are totally frozen, pinching them off the cluster in the same manner as unfrozen grapes.

About the Wines

The Cabernet Sauvignon is full bodied with a smooth velvety texture and a pleasing taste of berries that combines very well with the Cherry Chèvre Spread.

A refreshing white table wine, rich with fruit and with a dry, crisp finish, the Sauvignon Blanc is an excellent companion with the fettucini and chicken.

The Icewine & Brandy, produced nowhere else in the world, is a delicious blend of Vidal icewine and seven year-old brandy and is a wonderful way to complete a meal.

Opposite page: *Iced grapes with Chocolate Truffles and Icewine & Brandy*

ABOUT BARBARA GROEN

Barbara Groen is a food consultant for Kittling Ridge Estate Wines & Spirits. Barbara began her career in agricultural technology and has garnered a wealth of experience in food preparation and presentation through her extensive travels and studies around the world. While in residence in Singapore, she studied Asian cuisine and taught dessert classes. She further developed her talents in food styling during a three year period spent in San Francisco and the Bay area.

A Cozy Dinner Overlooking the Lake
KONZELMANN ESTATE WINERY

The Konzelmann family has marked the 100th anniversary of a family tradition of fine winemaking that dates back to 1893 in Uhlbach, near Stuttgart in Wuerttemberg, Germany. To celebrate this event, the Konzelmanns introduced a 1989 barrel-aged Johannisberg Riesling.

Friedrich Konzelmann's quest for innovation and quality in wines is being carried on today by his great grandson Herbert and great, great grandson Matthias. Herbert and Gudrun Konzelmann and their family emigrated to Canada in 1984, moving the Konzelmann winery from Germany to their new property on the shores of Lake Ontario near Niagara-On-The-Lake. Herbert was convinced that the climate and rich soil would be perfect for producing high quality wines. He found that the protection provided by the nearby escarpment and the resulting circulating air flow, combined with the moderating influ-

Left: *The Konzelmann Winery overlooking Lake Ontario.*

Right: *Herbert and Matthias Konzelmann.*

ence of the lake, creates warm days and cool nights. This prolongs the growing season which allows a late harvest, maximizing the fine acid balance and natural sugar content of the grapes, thus creating fuller-bodied wines. The morning dew and natural moisture from the lake provide delicate, unique and fruity characteristics in Konzelmann wines, similar to those of France's Alsace region.

Herbert introduced to Canada a system of vertical vine trellising and training, a method which allows the wind and sun to dry the morning dew from the vines more easily. It provides maximum exposure of the fruit and foliage to sunlight which helps secure an ideal sugar/ acid ratio in the mature fruit. This is not surprising. Herbert is both a perfectionist and a pioneer in the winemaking business. It's in his blood. His expertise in viticulture comes from a family lineage that dates back to 1521 on his mother's side. For 13 generations, grape growing and wine production have been carried on in his family. Herbert, a graduate of the famous Weinbau Schule in Weinsberg, Germany, had a long apprenticeship in winemaking. In 1987, he sent his son,

❧ MENU ❧

Smoked Fish, With Salad Garnish
Konzelmann 1992
Johannisberg Riesling

Roast Rack Of Lamb
With Finger Noodles
Konzelmann 1992 Chardonnay Reserve
or Konzelmann 1991 Late Harvest
Zweigelt

Fruit Gratin
Konzelmann 1991 Johannisberg
Riesling Late Harvest

Matthias, to Germany to apprentice at two vineyards. This also included part-time studies at a wine school. Matthias returned to Canada in 1990 to join his father as the fifth generation Konzelmann to work in the family business.

Although the Konzelmann reputation for quality has been established around the premium *vitis vinifera* grapes used in Europe's finest tradition wines, Herbert continues to search for new innovations. In fact, he was the first winemaker in the Niagara Peninsula to produce Riesling Traminer wine. Five acres are set aside where new varieties are tested for future commercial plants. While working to expand the range of wines, he and his family still maintain the tradition of picking some of their grapes by hand.

As part of their quality control, grapes used to make white wines undergo a long, cool fermentation period under controlled temperatures in stainless steel tanks. Red wines are also automatically temperature controlled using a sophisticated "Vino Top Fermenter" which helps to create softer, more velvety red wines.

The Konzelmann Estate Winery has won a number of national and international awards including the Grand Gold medal for their 1991 Vidal Icewine and a Gold medal for their 1991 Pinot Blanc at the VinItaly competition in Verona in 1993. This is the oldest and one of the largest competitions in the world.

Herbert Konzelmann and his family continue a wonderful tradition of quality, innovation and leadership into their family winery's second century.

Smoked Fish with Salad Garnish

FOR EACH PERSON SELECT:

- 2 shrimps, peeled and deveined (size-16/20 per lb [500 g])
- 2 scallops (size-under 20 per lb (500 g))
- 2 slices of smoked salmon or fillet of trout. Swordfish, mackerel or other fish could be used instead.

SALAD

- mixture of fresh, young garden greens
- clear dressing, such as one with Balsamic vinegar base
- chives
- 1 lemon and/or horseradish mustard or mayonnaise based sauce

This dish represents two courses in one, a cold fish appetizer and a salad course.

Smoked fish products are available in most fish shops, delicatessens or supermarkets with a specialty section. The alternative, for a superb, freshly smoked fish, is to do your own smoking. Very small portable smoking units—the size of a shoebox—are available.

If you smoke your own fish, brush both sides of the raw fish with a mixture of ½ lemon juice and ½ Worcestershire Sauce, salt and pepper. Allow to drip dry on a slanted surface or wire rack. Smoke according to directions which, depending on quantity of fish and heat source, is usually 10 to 15 minutes.

Lightly toss the mixture of garden greens with the clear dressing. Put a serving on each plate. Place the shrimps, scallops and a piece of fish around the greens. Decorate with chives, and serve with lemon wedges and/or horseradish.

Serve with the sauce of your choice for the fish or make your own.

Preparation time is about 15 minutes and only slightly longer if you smoke your own fish.

Roast Rack of Lamb with Finger Noodles

- 2 to 2¼ lbs (1000 to 1200 g) rack of fresh lamb, french styled
  salt, coarse freshly ground pepper
  sprigs of rosemary
- 4 tbsp (75 g) minced fresh garlic
- 4 coarsely cut onions
  sauce: mustard/brandy/cream, onion/garlic, peppercorn, or "au jus" from the roast
  fresh green beans
- 8 slices of bacon

FINGER NOODLES

- 1 lb (500 g) peeled and boiled potatoes

1 cup (120 g) all purpose flour
1 tbsp (20 g) cream of wheat
1 egg yolk
   salt and pepper to taste
   butter to sauté
1 bunch green onions
1 bunch fresh parsley

Preheat the oven to 400F (205°C). To prepare the lamb, rub with a mixture of salt, coarse freshly ground pepper, 1 tbsp (20 g) of minced fresh garlic, and sprigs of rosemary. If you prefer, you can use any other mix of preferred herbs and spices.

Place the lamb in a shallow, oven-proof dish or pie plate and place in oven. Bake for 15 minutes, then add 1 coarsely cut onion. Return to the oven. Check after 10 minutes and add a little water if required to prevent the onions from burning. Bake another 10 minutes and check to determine if roast is done to your liking. If you want to keep your roast warm while you finish preparing the noodles, reduce the oven temperature to 150F to 200F (66°C to 93°C) when the roast is rare.

To prepare the finger noodles, press the warm potatoes through a potato ricer. (You can get a ricer at almost any kitchen store. They are quite inexpensive.) Add the flour, cream of wheat and egg yolk. Shape the mixture into small finger sized noodles. Poach the noodles in simmering salt water until they float to the top. Then cool them in ice water, and allow to dry on a towel or paper towel. If you wish, you can prepare the noodles the day before to this point and refrigerate.

Sauté the noodles in butter until golden brown. Add finely chopped green onions a few minutes before serving. Remove the noodles to a warm platter and garnish with finely chopped, fresh parsley.

Slice the lamb and serve with your choice of sauce, the finger noodles, and fresh green beans garnished with freshly crumbled crispy bacon, finely chopped onions and garlic, and salt and pepper to taste.

Serves 4

Preparation time is approximately 1 hour.

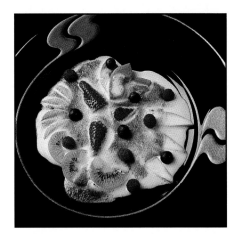

Fruit Gratin

Fresh or preserved fruits: peaches, strawberries, blueberries, raspberries, kiwi, poached pears or apricots to your liking may be used.

FOR CUSTARD
5 egg yolks
⅔ cup (100 g) icing sugar
   zest of 1/2 orange
   zest of 1/2 lemon
1 tbsp (15 to 20 mL) Grand Marnier
¾ cup (175 mL) 35% cream, whipped

For this dessert, avoid the use of hard fruits such as apples or raw pears. Peel, pit and slice fruit, as necessary. Place the fruit in a single layer on an oven-proof dessert plate. Mix or lay the fruit in a pattern.

To prepare the custard, place egg yolks, sugar, and orange and lemon zest in a bowl. Mix well with a whisk. Place the bowl on top of simmering water. A double boiler works well. Stir vigorously and constantly until slightly thickened. Do not overcook or it will curdle.

Remove the bowl from the water and continue to stir until cool. You can expedite the process by placing the bowl on ice. When lukewarm or cool, stir in the Grand Marnier, pour over the whipped cream, and gently fold in the custard.

Partially cover the fruit plate arrangement with the custard cream, exposing some of the fruit. Place the plate under a broiler or a pre-heated oven with the top element on full, until golden brown. Dust with icing sugar.

Serves 4

Preparation time is approximately 45 minutes.

✄ About the Wines ✄

Chef Emil Rinderlin says his choice of Konzelmann Johannisberg Riesling for the smoked fish works very well.

"Although it is difficult to match beyond 'wellness' any wine with smoked fish and a light mustard sauce, combined with a clear salad dressing, we fared very well with the Johannisberg Riesling.

"Fish dishes of a delicate nature such as trout, dover sole or salmon demand a soft wine to avoid overpowering the fish. Smoking this fish, however, and serving with a piquant sauce allows us to complement this dish with the Riesling."

According to Emil, the roast rack of lamb permits an opportunity to be adventurous in choosing either a red or white wine so he chose one of each. "I chose Konzelmann Late Harvest Zweigelt because it is a velvety, full and aromatic wine which supports the lamb wonderfully."

One of Emil's favourite wines is Konzelmann Chardonnay Reserve. "Fruity in character and the right amount of acidity with a subtle toasted wood flavour, this dry white wine harmonizes well with the lamb."

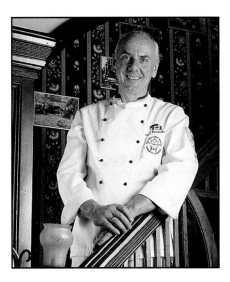

CHEF EMIL RINDERLIN

Since 1981, Emil has been the chef-owner of Rinderlins Diningrooms in Welland, Ontario, recognized as one of the finest restaurants in the Niagara area. He is also the managing partner of Carnival Food Fair/Jamz Bistro and Bar at Ontario Place in Toronto.

Emil began his chef training in Europe, where he worked in Germany and Switzerland before coming to Canada in 1967. He is a former silver medal winner at the World Culinary Exhibition and Competition, where there were participants from over 30 countries.

Emil has played an important role in promoting tourism hospitality in the Niagara area through his involvement in a number of associations and task forces, and has been very supportive of the development of the Niagara wine industry.

Christopher Newton

Christopher Newton has long been recognized as one of Canada's outstanding artistic directors. He has been Artistic Director of the Shaw Festival in Niagara-On-The-Lake for 15 seasons and has directed many of the company's major works. Some of these have included Misalliance, Saint Joan, You Never Can Tell, Pygmalion, and Caesar and Cleopatra.

Over the years, Christopher has directed or performed for most major theatres across Canada. He has worked in television and film as well, and is a well-known radio broadcaster. He has also written several stage plays which have been produced by several theatres across Canada. Christopher is also an Honorary Fellow of the Royal Conservatory of Music in Toronto.

As an actor, he has performed with the Canadian Players, the National Arts Centre, the Vancouver Playhouse and the Stratford Festival in Canada. He has also performed on Broadway. Some of his memorable characterizations at the Shaw Festival included the Noel Coward sophisticates of *Private Lives* and *Present Laughter*, Captain Hook in *Peter Pan*, and the poker-faced cowlicked butler in *Charlie's Aunt*.

In 1977, Christopher was awarded the Queen's Silver Jubilee Medal and, in 1986, he received the Dora Award for Best Direction of a Musical, for the Shaw Festival's production of The Dessert Song. Christopher enjoys cooking in his beautiful home in Niagara-On-The-Lake. The Gazpacho soup is one of his summer favourites.

🜚 About the Wines 🜚

The Henry of Pelham Blanc de Noir Cabernet Franc and Stoney Ridge Cellars Romance, two wines with full fruit flavour and pleasant lingering tastes, are an excellent match for the gazpacho soup.

Gazpacho Soup

6 cups (1.3 L) tomato juice (an ordinary large can)
5 tbsp (85 mL) salad oil
4 tbsp (75 mL) red wine vinegar
1 tsp (5 g) salt
1 tsp (5 g) sugar

Then real vegetables, and this is where it gets dicey.
1 big cucumber

1 big onion
1 green pepper
2 or 3 large tomatoes (skin these — that is, drop them in boiling water until the skins crack, then just peel them off.)
2 cloves of garlic
some parsley
pepper

Worcestershire sauce — I use quite a lot, some people use celery. A bit of dill is also good.

All you do is put all of this together in a blender and puree coarsely. You put it in sealed jars and let it sit in the fridge for a day or two to get rid of the bubbles. Not really "cooking", this is "making". Still, it tastes good in the summer.

69

A Real Country Dinner

LAKEVIEW CELLARS
ESTATE WINERY

For Lorraine and Eddie Gurinskas, owning a farm and winery in the beautiful rolling hills of Vineland in Niagara has been an act of true love.

It would have to be. Each weekend for three years they commuted from Ottawa to Vineland - about six hours each way - to work on their 13 acre farm. Eddie was an employee of the Canadian National Railways and an award winning amateur wine maker and, until he retired, they worked the farm, including harvesting the grapes and selling them to local Niagara wineries. They had no thought of opening

their own winery until they moved permanently to Vineland and realized the growth potential of the Niagara wine industry.

Then the challenge began. They had to build a wine boutique, tasting room and office in the winery building next to their home. When they officially opened Lakeview Cellars in the Spring of 1991 they had no idea of what to expect in terms of consumer response to their wines and potential sales. There was certainly no need to worry. In their first year of operation they won awards for their wines and haven't looked back since.

They produce 11 different wines, most of them white and including a Vidal Icewine. The winery is open for tours and tastings, and you know that when you visit Lakeview Cellars, Eddie or Lorraine will be there to greet you personally.

❧ MENU ❧

Sweet Potato and Scottish Smoked Salmon Soup
Lakeview Cellars 1992 Pinot Gris

Sweetbreads in Port Wine Butter Sauce
Lakeview Cellars 1992 Cabernet Sauvignon

Caramelized Apple Tart Tatin
Lakeview Cellars 1992 Vidal Icewine

Sweet Potato and Scottish Smoked Salmon Soup

¾ lb (400 g) sweet potatoes, peeled and cubed
¼ cup (50 g) shallots, peeled and diced
¼ lb (150 g) smoked Scottish salmon, cut in pieces
1¼ cup (300 mL) light fish stock
2¾ cup (600 mL) 35% cream
1 tbsp (15 g) chervil
¾ oz (20 g) smoked salmon for individual plate garnish
salt, pepper to taste
2 tbsp (30 g) butter for sautéeing

Sauté shallots and sweet potatoes in butter. Add the salmon and fish stock and bring to a boil. Add the cream and let simmer until potatoes are soft. Purée in blender and season with salt and pepper.

Before serving soup, add the chopped chervil and garnish with strips of smoked salmon and one chervil sprig.

Serves 4.

Preparation time is approximately 30 minutes.

Sweetbreads in Port Wine Butter Sauce with Zucchini, Carrot Rosti, Vegetables, Apples

4 cups (1 L) veal demi glace (recipe in glossary)
2¾ cups (600 g) sweetbreads, blanched and cleaned, broken into small pieces
¾ cup (200 mL) Port wine
2 tbsp (40 g) shallots
½ cup (120 g) iced butter cubes
2 tbsp (40 g) butter
salt, pepper to taste

For this recipe, the glace de viande needs to be prepared the day before it is served.

Sauté sweetbreads in butter, add shallots, and caramelize. Add the Port wine, flambé and simmer for approximately 2 minutes. Remove sweetbreads and keep warm.

Add veal demi glace and let reduce to ½. Add the iced butter cubes and let melt while stirring. Add the sweetbreads to the sauce and toss.

Zucchini and Carrot Rosti

¼ lb (100 g) carrots, peeled and ruffled (grated)

¼ lb (100 g) zucchini, washed, ends cut off and ruffled

¼ lb (100 g) potatoes, half way cooked, peeled and ruffled

1½ tbsp (20 g) butter
   salt, pepper to taste

1 apple

1½ tbsp (30 g) sugar

Mix everything together, then season and put into ring cutter in teflon pan with butter. Fry until golden brown. Take out of the pan with a spatula and put on plate. Remove ring cutter.

Glaze in butter and caramelized sugar the vegetable, turned apples, zucchini, carrots, salt and pepper.

Serves 4

Preparation time is approximately 30 minutes, but remember to make the glace de viande the day before.

Caramelized Apple Tart Tatin

3 to 4 lbs (1.35 to 1.8 kg) apples

½ cup (115 g) sugar, granulated

2 tbsp (25 g) butter
   parchment paper

Short dough pastry

½ cup (110 g) butter, unsalted

⅓ cup (85 g) shortening, Crisco

½ cup (110 g) sugar, granulated

1 whole egg

1¼ cup (140 g) all purpose flour

Whip butter, shortening, sugar and egg together until creamy. Now add flour slowly just until flour and fats are incorporated. Refrigerate for about ½ hour.

Peel and core 3 to 4 lbs (1.35 to 1.8 kg) of apples and cut into quarters. Line an 8 inch (20 cm) flan pan or sponge pan with parchment paper. Sprinkle ½ cup (110 g) of granulated sugar and arrange the quartered apples in concentric circles. Repeat the layers of apples and sugar three times. Take about 2 tbsp (25 g) of butter and place

dots of butter on each of the sugar apples. Roll out the sweet dough and cut a ring by using the outer edge of the sponge pan and place the sweet dough on top. Make sure that the fruit is contained within the lid.

Bake at 450F (230°C) for 30 to 35 minutes. Place a serving dish on top of the flan and turn over. Remove and sprinkle with dusted icing sugar. If you wish, serve with fresh cream or ice cream.

Serves 8

Preparation time is about 1 hour.

Above: *Lorraine and Eddie Gurinskas*

About the Wines

Lorraine Gurinskas of Lakeview explains the choice of wines:

"The 1992 Pinot Gris has a lovely floral bouquet and a light fruity flavour. It is a very clean, fresh, crisp, dry wine and marries very well with the sweet potato and Scottish smoked salmon soup.

"To accompany the sweetbreads in Port wine butter sauce, the 1992 Cabernet Sauvignon has a slight, smokey, fruity bouquet, and cherry flavour. It is a soft wine with good body, easy tannins and is well balanced.

"The 1992 Vidal Icewine, which is matched with the caramelized apple tart tatin, has a rich amber colour, a pronounced bouquet of apricots, rich luscious sweetness and good acidity."

CHEF RALPH BRETZIGHEIMER

Ralph received most of his training as a chef in Germany where he completed a traditional German apprenticeship program. He worked as a chef in major hotels in Germany before joining Mövenpick as a sous chef in 1986.

In 1988, he moved to Toronto to work in Mövenpick's restaurant in Yorkville. In 1990 he was promoted to executive chef. He joined the Pillar and Post Inn, a five star resort hotel with full conference facilities in Niagara-On-The-Lake, as executive chef in 1994.

When he is not working, he enjoys fishing, motorcycles, and wine tasting. With those pastimes, it's not surprising that Ralph likes living in the Niagara Region.

A Summer Supper in the Country

MARYNISSEN ESTATES

It was a wine expert from Paris who wanted to take home only award winning Marynissen from a major wine show in Niagara and the persuasive arguments of his two daughters that convinced John Marynissen to open a small commercial winery in 1991.

Instead of retiring at the age of 65, John began a new career and says that he feels 10 years younger today. It was not a difficult transition. John and his wife Adriana emigrated to Canada from Holland in 1952 and have been growing grapes on their farm ever since. In fact, he supplied Donald Ziraldo and Karl Kaiser with their Marechal Foch grapes when Inniskillin applied for their wine license 20 years ago.

John Marynissen was the first grape grower in Canada to plant Cabernet Sauvignon and is considered by many wine experts to produce the best French oak-aged Cabernet Sauvignon in the country. In his amateur days he won many awards including the Best of Show for his 1989 Chardonnay at the American Wine Society's annual North American Wine Competition. John's amateur wine competitors were probably pleased to see him turn professional because his entries often discouraged them from any hope of winning. At one competition alone he entered six wines and won four gold medals.

In making deep, complex red wines he uses the same process as the French makers of Nouveau Beaujolais. The carbonic maceration process is used to ferment half of the grapes that go into his Cabernet Sauvignon and Merlot wines, a method of leaving the grapes whole and letting them ferment in a sealed container. The juice is naturally squeezed out by the pressure of the grapes being piled together. The result is a superb concentration of flavour.

The Marynissen winery business is a family affair. While John produces the wine, his son Tom manages the farm and Sandra handles the administrative and marketing. Adriana can often be found talking to visitors and providing tastings in their wine boutique. It's an enjoyable experience to taste Marynissen wine and to converse and laugh with other visitors while everyone sits at their huge oak table in the wine boutique.

Warm Quail Salad

4 quails, deboned
1 radicchio
1 Belgium endive
1 curly endive
1 romaine lettuce
freshly ground black pepper

DRESSING
Balsamic vinegar
extra virgin olive oil
2 shallots, chopped finely
1 tsp (5 g) of grain mustard

Wash and dry the greens, then set aside. Prepare dressing and put on stove to warm. Dredge quail in flour and pan fry quickly in oil over high heat until just golden. Arrange lettuce on plates. Place quail on lettuce and pour warm dressing on top. Finish with freshly ground black pepper.

Make the dressing by mixing 5 parts of oil to 1 part of vinegar. Left over will keep in the refrigerator.

Serves 4

Preparation time is about 20 minutes.

❧ MENU ❧

Warm Quail Salad
Marynissen 1992 barrel fermented
Chardonnay

Stuffed Roast Leg of Rabbit
Marynissen 1991 Cabernet Merlot

Poached Pears in Chocolate Sauce
Marynissen 1991 Pinot Noir

Stuffed Roast Leg of Rabbit

2 3 lb (1.5 kg) rabbits
   pork fat or bacon
   sage, thyme, parsley, to taste
   salt and black pepper, to taste
   crepenetti (sausage casing)

FOR STOCK

1 bunch carrots
1 bunch celery
3 bay leaves
2 onions
2 red peppers

Begin making stock first by combining in a pot 18 cups (4 L) of water carrots, rabbit or veal bones, celery, bay leaves, onions, peppers and herbs. Simmer for approximately 4 hours, strain and skim, and reduce to 2 cups (500 mL).

To prepare rabbits, remove loins and legs from each rabbit. Each will divide into two portions. Debone top of each leg, leaving skin-bone in. (If you prefer, you can purchase boned out rabbits at specialty butcher shops). Roll each loin in herbs, garlic, salt and pepper and wrap with pork fat. Stuff into empty leg cavity. Wrap entire leg with crepenetti. Bake rabbit at 350F (180°C) for 20 minutes.

Before serving, add more chopped herbs and whisk in a nut of butter to the stock.

Serves 4

Preparation time: allow 4 hours to simmer stock. Otherwise, time to prepare is approximately 30 minutes.

Opposite page: *Warm quail salad*

Above: *A view of the Niagara Escarpment*

Left: *Stuffed roast leg of rabbit*

Above: *Poached pears in chocolate sauce.*

Right: *Sandra, Adriana and John Marynissen.*

Poached Pears in Chocolate Sauce

4 pears
2½ cups (600 g) sugar
4½ cups (1 L) water
3 cloves
½ cinnamon stick
   juice from one lemon
   raspberries (optional)

CHOCOLATE SAUCE
¾ cup (170 g) plain chocolate
   large knob of butter
3 tsp (15 mL) heavy cream
1 tbsp (20 g) instant coffee

Combine water, sugar, cloves, cinnamon, lemon juice. Bring to a boil and then turn down to simmer. Peel and core pears and add to syrup. Simmer until tender. Remove with a slotted spoon and let cool slightly.

Melt chocolate over hot water. Add remaining ingredients and heat gently until melted and warm. Beat well.

Cover plates with chocolate sauce, arrange pears in middle and garnish with raspberries.

Serves 4

Preparation time is approximately 1 hour.

About the Wines

Chef Mark Walpole chose flavourful lettuces, a minimum of vinegar in the dressing, and a suitable tasty meat to produce a warm salad which has an excellent balance with the wood overtones in the 1992 Barrel Fermented Chardonnay.

Mark and Sandra Marynissen teamed up to choose the 1991 Cabernet Merlot, a full bodied wine with a soft finish, because it matches well with the milder taste of rabbit meat and complements the many flavours of the sauce.

In choosing a light red wine with dessert, Mark and Sandra wanted to try something different. They chose the 1991 Pinot Noir because it stands up to the strong taste of the chocolate and balances well with the fruitiness of the pear. An excellent choice.

CHEF MARK WALPOLE

Mark is a native of the Niagara Region. He is from St. Catharines, Ontario and a graduate of the chef training program at George Brown College in Toronto. Mark is a Certified Chef de Cuisine and has worked for the past 10 years at the Prince of Wales Hotel, a wonderful, large old inn in downtown Niagara-On-The-Lake with full conference facilities.

He works extensively with local Niagara wineries and develops Canadian cuisine menus using local produce and game that include quail, pheasant, and rabbit.

Dinner on the Winery Patio
PILLITTERI ESTATES WINERY

For Gary Pillitteri, the opening of Pillitteri Estates Winery in June, 1993 was the culmination of a lifetime dream. Since arriving in Canada from his native Sicily in 1948, and through many years as a grape grower in Niagara and amateur winemaker, he had dreamed of that moment.

The turning point took place five years earlier when Gary won a gold medal for his icewine in Niagara's amateur wine competition. He knew then he could make his dream come true. But he had been thinking about early retirement and could only build a professional and high-quality winery with the expertise and full commitment of his family. They were behind him all the way. This is a real family business. Gary's son Charles is general manager; son-in-law Jamie Slingerland is public relations director and manages the family vineyards; daughters Connie and Lucy and Lucy's husband Helmut Friesen are sales representatives. And Gary's wife Lena runs everything. The family decided to bring in a professional winemaker, Joe Will. Joe is a graduate of Roseworthy, the prestigious wine school in Australia, and has more than 10 years' experience in winemaking.

Their grapes are primarily harvested from the family's 140 acres of farms, which include 40 acres of vineyards in Niagara-On-The-Lake, with production 100 per cent Ontario

vinifera and French hybrid grapes. Initially, the winery produced a variety of red and white wines including two house wines, Chariot Red and Chariot White, named after the Pillitteri logo — a stylized Sicilian cart (see photo inset). The original antique stands in the winery's reception area. They have gradually been adding to their production with new varietal and icewines. Total winery production is about 70,000 litres but can be expanded to 100,000. Their goal is to produce 100 per cent VQA varietal wines.

Pillitteri Estates Winery has a delightful outdoor wine garden patio and a large hospitality room where a variety of events are held. There is also an opportunity for one-stop shopping. Adjacent to the winery is a bakery and greenhouse, as well as the seasonal farm market and fruit packing plant that the family has operated for over two decades. During the season, visitors can take a trolley ride through the vineyards and orchards, a walking tour of the winery and participate in formal tasting lessons.

For Gary Pillitteri, there's no talk now of early retirement. "What retirement," he says. "I'm having too much fun." The story could end there and it would be a remarkable dream come true, but it goes on. In 1993 Gary was elected to Parliament as a Member of the governing Liberal Party, the culmination of a second lifetime dream. It must be a fantasy!

Sea Scallops Wrapped in Filo Pastry with Ginger and a Citrus Beurre Blanc

16 sea scallops
1 sheet filo pastry
   clarified butter (or olive oil)
1 ginger root
   oven dried tomato and chives, for garnish
   salt and cayenne pepper, to taste

FOR BEURRE BLANC
4 shallots
½ lb (225 g) butter
2 tbsp (30 mL) white wine vinegar
¼ cup (30 mL) white wine
¼ cup (30 mL) fish stock (optional flavour)
2 tbsp (30 mL) whipping cream
   juice and zest of lemon

Cut the ginger into small cubes (brunoise), then blanch in boiling water for 5 minutes to remove sharpness.

To prepare scallops, take one sheet of filo pastry and brush with clarified butter, or olive oil, then fold in half and brush the top side. Cut the filo pastry into 4 squares. Put 1 scallop in the middle of each square, sprinkle on some ginger, and add salt and cayenne pepper to taste. Fold up the 4 corners to form a purse around the scallop and do the same with each until finished. Bake in oven at 350F (180°C) until golden brown.

For the beurre blanc, finely chop the shallots and cook in a pan until translucent. Add the wine, stock and vinegar. Reduce by ¾, then add 2 tbsp (30 mL) of whipping cream and bring to a boil. Whisk in the cold butter (cut into pieces), but do not let boil again. Squeeze in the juice of the lemon.

Strain off the shallots and add the zest of the lemon.

Place sauce on each plate, arrange scallops and garnish with chives, oven-dried tomato and some left over ginger.

Serves 4

Preparation time is about 30 minutes.

Magret of Muscovy Duck with a Morel Mushroom and Blackberry Glaze

4 breasts of duck
   morel mushrooms, small handful
1 pint (500 mL) blackberries
2 tbsp (30 mL) cassis
1½ cup (350 mL) veal demi glace
2 tbsp (30 g) butter
   salt and pepper, to taste

Above: *Magret of Muscovy Duck*
Right: *The Winery Boutique*

The veal demi glace takes a long time to prepare and should be cooked at least a day in advance. Gently boil veal bones and natural gelatin for several hours along with some roasted vegetables and herbs to add flavour. Then strain the bones hrough a sieve to leave only pure stock. Reduce the stock by heavy boiling until a demi glace is achieved. The stock must be monitored constantly as it reduces, in order to skim off the impurities.

In a frying pan, cook breasts with skin side down for 5 minutes over medium heat. Then turn over and cook for another 3 minutes. Turn the breasts back on skin side and place in oven for 10 minutes at 450F (230°C) to reach medium rare.

For the sauce, add morel mushrooms, fresh blackberries, and a dash of cassis to the demiglace. Just before serving, whisk in 2 tbsp (30 mL) of butter.

To accompany the duck, Chef Antony Nuth served a collection of vegetables and potato, including spinach, red cabbage, corn, asparagus, baby turnip, red pepper, carrot and new potato.

Serves 4

Preparation time, not including the demi glace which needs to be prepared at least a day in advance, is approximately 30 minutes.

Tarte au Citron with Raspberry Coulis and Cassis Sorbet

Makes one tarte in a 12 inch (30 cm) flan ring

FOR LEMON MIX
1½	lb (650 g) sweet pastry
5	lemons
10	eggs
2	cups (375 g) sugar
1⅓	cups (325 mL) whipping cream

FOR SWEET PASTRY
2	cups (250 g) flour
¾	cup (200 g) butter
⅔	cup (100 g) icing sugar
2	egg yolks
¼	cup (50 mL) whipping cream

FOR RASPBERRY COULIS
1 pint (500 mL) raspberries
½ cup (100 mL) sugar stock (¼ cup [50 g] of sugar to ¼ cup [50 mL] of water)

To prepare the lemon mix, whisk the eggs and sugar until dissolved. Remove the zest and juice from the lemons and whisk them into the mixture. Semi-whip the cream and fold it in. The mix should be prepared 24 hours in advance. Just before using, whisk it back together with a wire whisk.

To prepare the sweet pasty, mix the flour and butter together thoroughly. Sift in the icing sugar and add the salt. Then add the egg yolks and cream. Work it only until the liquids are incorporated or the dough may become tough. Put in refrigerator for 2 hours.

Roll out the dough with rolling pin ¼ inch (6 mm) thick. Place in flan ring and push into corners, letting excess over hang. It can be trimmed after it is cooked. Blind bake the pastry using tin foil and placing beans or rice to fill the flan. When the pastry is cooked, take out the foil with the beans or rice. Pour the whisked lemon mix into flan and bake for 35 to 40 minutes at 325F to 350F (160 to 180°C) until set. Be certain that there are no holes in the pastry.

For the raspberry coulis, put 1 pint (500 mL) of raspberries in blender with ½ cup (100 mL) of sugar stock. Blend them, then strain to remove seeds.

Put a spoonful of cassis sorbet on each plate with the tarte.

Serves 4

Preparation time is approximately 1 hour, not including advance preparation or refrigeration time for sweet pastry.

CHEF ANTONY NUTH

Born in Ottawa, Ontario, Antony spent a large part of his youth as a successful modern pentathalon athlete. Working in a local restaurant to help fund his athletics, he realized how much he enjoyed the business. Antony spent 5 years in London and Paris working as a chef's apprentice before returning to Canada in 1990.

In 1992 Antony and his co-owner, partner, Richard Marshall, opened Herbs, a very successful new classic French style restaurant in Toronto, which offers a daily changing menu using only fresh market produce.

🏵 About the Wines 🏵

The Dry Riesling, with its slightest trace of sweetness and refreshing finish, is an excellent match with the scallops wrapped in filo pastry.

The Cabernet Sauvigon is a lighter weight wine which complements the duck. If you prefer a white wine, the oak aged Chardonnay, with the light citrus and apple of the Chardonnay grape, matches well with this dish.

Top Left: *Winemakers Joe Will and Charles Pillitteri*

Photos: *Views of the Reif Cellars*

A Summertime Sunday Supper

R E I F   E S T A T E   W I N E R Y

In the eighteenth century the location of the Reif winery was a stagecoach stop for travellers going from Newark (now Niagara-On-The-Lake) to Queenston (home of Laura Secord) along the banks of the Niagara River. This historical significance is not lost on the Reif family, who began their own tradition of winemaking more than 100 years ago in Germany's Rhine Region.

Emigrating to Niagara-On-The-Lake in 1977, the Reif family planted European vinifera vines over the next five years and brought winemaking equipment from the Reif winery in Neustadt. The traditional Reif philosophy that "nature makes wine" is carried on in Canada where every effort is made to limit interference in this delicate process. By pruning and thinning vines Reif produces a small yield of excellent quality. This thinning technique combined with an intentionally extended season produces a very flavorful fruit.

Reif uses both French and American oak barriques, stainless steel tanks and German oak casks to mature the wine.

Reif's unique policy of using 100 percent estate

grown grapes follows another family tradition adhered to for over a century. Among their wide selection is a new premium line featuring unfiltered Cabernet Sauvignon and Merlot. Since the wine is not filtered, it retains its full body and complexity. It is specially wax sealed and packaged in clear cellophane so it can be placed in cellars for many years and sold as a special vintage wine. Purchasers are invited to sign a registry for each numbered bottle.

Reif is a small family-run operation. Klaus Reif, a Geisenheim Wine University graduate in viticulture and oenology, guides all aspects of production at the winery. Sabina Reif handles the sales and other areas of administration. Visitors to the Reif winery are made to feel very comfortable. The staff is very personable and helpful. And their commitment doesn't stop with making wonderful wines. In the Reif Gallery of Contemporary Canadian art, the focus is on the contemporary fine arts of the Niagara Region, and from other parts of Canada, adding to the full enjoyment of a visit to the Reif Estate winery.

⚜ MENU ⚜

Smoked Venison with Mango Red Currant Sauce
Reif 1992 Cabernet Franc

Fillet of Salmon with Maple Dijon Orange Sauce
Reif 1993 Johannisberg Riesling Medium Dry

Summer Berry Pudding
Reif 1992 Vidal Icewine

Smoked Venison with Mango Red Currant Sauce

FOR EACH PERSON:
- ¼ lb (115 g) smoked venison
- 1 radicchio leaf
- 1 curly endive leaf
- 3 Belgium endive leaves
- ⅓ cup (85 mL) mango purée
- ¼ cup (50 g) fresh red currants (or canned)
- 1 pk pea sprouts

Slice the smoked venison very thinly and lay ¼ lb (115 g) on each plate. Arrange leaves on the plate to decorate. Mix mango purée with whole red currants very carefully, meaning don't crush. Place pea sprouts amongst the leaves to give a splash of colour and pour sauce in the middle of venison.

Serves 4

Preparation time is about 15 minutes.

Fillet of Salmon with Maple Dijon Orange Sauce

- ⅓ lb (170 g) salmon, cleaned, filleted and deboned per person
- 1 cup (250 mL) Dijon
- 1 cup (250 mL) maple syrup
- ½ cup (115 g) brown sugar
- 1½ cups (350 mL) orange juice
- 1½ cups (350 mL) fish stock
- ½ cup (100 mL) dry white wine

Left: *Smoked Venison with Mango Red Currant Sauce*

Right: *Fillet of Salmon with Maple Dijon Orange Sauce*

Prepare the orange sauce first, either the day before and refrigerate, or earlier the same day. To prepare the orange sauce, place orange juice in a pan with the fish stock and white wine. Reduce by three quarters and then add ¼ cup (50 mL) of maple syrup. It should coat the back of a spoon. If not, reduce a little more.

Cut and clean the salmon fillets. Place the fillets on an oiled baking sheet. Mix Dijon, brown sugar and ¾ cup (175 mL) of maple syrup together in a bowl and then place mixture over each salmon to coat each piece. Bake at 375F (190°C) for 25 minutes or until firm to the touch.

Place the orange sauce around the salmon fillets.

Serves 4

Preparation time is approximately 1½ hours, unless you prepare the orange sauce ahead, which is a good idea.

Summer Berry Pudding

1 loaf of sliced white bread, crusts removed
    sugar or honey to taste
1 pint (575 g) sliced strawberries
1 pint (575 g) raspberries
1 pint (575 g) cranberries
1 pint (575 g) blueberries
6 apples, peeled, cored and sliced
4½ cups (1 L) orange juice

Cover the bottom and sides of a springform pan with plastic wrap. Tightly fit the sliced bread to cover the bottom of the pan. Place orange zest and juice in a pan with honey or sugar. It should be sweet but not too sweet. Add berries and apples and bring to a boil. Take off the stove and strain the juice, reserving it for the sauce. Place about ¼ inch (5mm) of fruit mixture on bread so it is covered; layer more bread on top; and continue to alternate layers of fruit and bread until there are 4 or 5 layers. Cover the pudding with plastic wrap, place a plate on top to fit the pan, place something heavy on top and put in refrigerator overnight.

Now bring the juice to a boil and thicken with corn starch. Don't make too thick.

Take out of springform pan, cut a wedge and place on each plate. Pour some sauce over top of pudding. Serve with whipped cream if you wish and garnish with fresh fruit.

Serves 4

Preparation time is about 1½ hours. It is best to make this dessert the day before.

🌿 About the Wines 🌿

In conjunction with winemaker Klaus Reif, Graeme Gatenby-Wilson chose the Cabernet Franc with the smoked venison because it is a full bodied wine that matches well with the red meat. In addition, the dominant flavors of black cherries and black currants in the wine stand up well to the gamey, heavy flavor of the venison.

The Johannisberg Riesling medium dry is full fruit, predominantly grapefruit, with a noticeable hint of residual sweetness which matches very well with the sweet glaze and spicy taste of the salmon.

The aroma of the Vidal Icewine is rich with apricots and honey and has a full bodied taste with a long, lingering finish which is particularly well suited to the pudding which is made with all natural berries and no added sugar.

Right: *Klaus and Sabina Reif*

CHEF GRAEME GATENBY-WILSON

Graeme has been a strong proponent of Canadian cuisine for many years and in the last five has focused his attention on gaining Canada appropriate recognition.

Graeme graduated in hotel management from Torquay Technical College in South Devon, England and went on to take his City and Guilds and won Apprentice of the Year in 1971. He worked in Switzerland for two years before emigrating to Canada. He has been Executive Sous Chef to Daniel Dunas, the Chef to Winston Churchill and also to Pierre Trudeau. Chef Graeme has also served the Royal Family in England.

Since 1988, he has been working in Niagara-On-The-Lake and is employed at the White Oaks Inn. The Inn is a luxury resort nestled at the foot of the Niagara Escarpment with conference facilities and a full fitness and racquet club.

Jonathan Welsh

Jonathan Welsh is one of Canada's most successful actors. His starring role in the hit series *E.N.G.*, which appeared on television stations around the world, marked his fourth regular role on a Canadian network television series.

Born in the City of St. Catharines, Ontario, Jonathan began his entertainment career after moving to Toronto where he starred in such wonderful theatre productions as *Godspell*, *Hamlet* and *You Can't Take It With You*. He was also a member of the cast of Canada's production of *Hair*. Following his successful career in theatre, he moved into the world of television and film.

In addition to his acting career, Jonathan created and runs Performers for Literacy, a group designed to encourage parents to take an active interest in their children's reading skills and to help develop them. The group has opened The

Second Story, a permanent storefront location at a mall in Toronto, where a variety of storytellers - from film stars to firefighters - read stories to parents and their children and encourage them to read together.

"Although we're trying to influence parents through their children, we would also like to reach more parents directly through parent-teacher associations and readings in malls," Jonathan explains.

Jonathan and his wife Heather, his two daughters Hilary and Julia, and his son Owen, enjoy seafood and pasta. Since they have such a busy schedule, this recipe, which can be prepared quickly, is one of their favourites.

About the Wines

For Jonathan's seafood pasta, Inniskillin Wines Pinot Noir matches very well, or if you prefer a white wine, Hillebrand Harvest Classics Chardonnay is an excellent choice with this dish.

A Summer Vegetable and Seafood Pasta

¾ lb (400 g) uncooked prawns, shelled and deveined

⅔ lb (300 g) Asian noodles (or linguini, fettucini, or other noodles of your choice)

1 eggplant

2 zucchini

3 tomatoes

¼ cup (50 mL) lemon juice

¼ cup (50 mL) olive oil

½ tbsp (10 g) sugar

½ tbsp (10 g) thyme

½ tbsp (10 g) black peppercorns

4 garlic cloves

Cut eggplant and zucchini into long slices, and peel and slice tomatoes. Heat olive oil in pan. Turn down to medium heat and add eggplant and zucchini. Stir for several minutes until vegetables are cooked but still firm. Add tomatoes, lemon juice, sugar, thyme and peppercorns and stir occasionally for 5 minutes.

Add prawns and crushed garlic cloves and stir over low heat, or about 4 minutes, until prawns are just cooked.

Cook noodles in large pan of boiling water until tender. Drain and stir noodles into the pan with vegetables and prawns. Serve immediately.

Serves 4

Preparation time is about 20 minutes.

A Niagara Dinner for Four

STONECHURCH VINEYARDS

L ocal folklore has it that during Prohibition smugglers rowed up McNab Creek from Lake Ontario and stored contraband rum in caves under an historic church now referred to as "Stonechurch", after which Stonechurch Vineyards is named.

Since 1972, the Hunse family has been planting and developing vineyards in one of the best winegrowing areas in Niagara, close to the moderating effects of Lake Ontario. In 1990 they opened Stonechurch Vineyards. About half of their 200 acre farm is now planted exclusively in *vitis vinifera* and hybrid grape varieties.

Facilities at Stonechurch include an hospitality room with a fireplace that can accommodate up to 100 visitors. An adjacent patio is an excellent area to enjoy the surrounding vineyards. For those who want a closer look at the vineyards, tours are available on Stonechurch vintage tractors.

Apart from local distribution of their wines, Stonechurch has exported its wines to Europe and the Far East. Future international markets include distribution in the United States, Mexico and the United Kingdom. Richard, Frances and the rest of their family are proud to be part of the growing Canadian wine industry as it matures in the world market. Maturity has come quickly for the industry in general and for Stonechurch in particular. Stonechurch Vineyards won a Grand Gold medal at the 1994 VinItaly international wine competition in Verona, Italy for their 1991 Icewine, an enormous achievement for a small, boutique winery. The Grand

Opposite: *Mechanical harvester picking grapes in Stonechurch vineyards*

 97

Gold is the highest medal awarded in the competition by 90 international judges, many of whom include internationally renowned winemakers.

In its tasteful wine boutique in Niagara, Stonechurch Vineyards offers more than 12 of its quality wines from the bold Baco Noir to the delicate and fruity Gewurztraminer. While Stonechurch prospers and expands, it continues to be a warm, hospitable place to visit.

🌿 MENU 🌿

Terrine Of Foie Gras Marinated In Icewine,
served with a poached Niagara peach and baby green salad
Stonechurch Vineyards 1992 Riesling

A Duo Of Canadian Venison
in a Stonechurch Vineyards Cabernet Sauvignon and blueberry jus
Stonechurch Vineyards 1992 Cabernet Sauvignon

Icewine Semifreddo in a buckwheat and pistachio wafer
with valhrona chocolate Zabaglione

Terrine of Foie Gras Marinated in Icewine served with a poached Niagara peach and baby green salad

TERRINE OF FOIE GRAS
2¼ lbs (1.1 kg) duck foie gras
3½ tbsp (60 mL) icewine
2 tbsp (40 mL) V.S.O.P. Cognac
salt and pepper to taste

POACHED PEACHES
4 cups (1 L) water
2 cups (450 g) sugar
2 fresh peaches, halved
½ cinnamon stick
juice of 2 lemons

BABY GREENS
1 head frisé
1 head baby oak leaf
1 head baby lollo rossa
1 head Boston lettuce
1 small radicchio

DRESSING FOR SALAD

⅓ cup (75 mL) extra virgin olive oil
3 tbsp (40 mL) raspberry vinegar
2 shallots, finely chopped
½ pint (300 g) raspberries
  salt and pepper to taste
1 bunch chives, finely chopped
1 bunch chervil

Devein the foie gras and season with salt and pepper. Marinate for 24 hours in the icewine, cognac mixture. Layer the foie gras in a 2.5 inch by 3 inch by 10 inch (6 cm by 7.5 cm by 25 cm) terra cotta terrine. Press down gently on the foie gras to make the surface level and cover with aluminium foil.

Place the terrine in water bath, with water level 1 inch (2.5 cm) below the top of the terrine. Bake in a preheated oven at 350F (180°C) for 40 minutes. Remove terrine from water, uncover and allow to cool at room temperature for 30 minutes.

Cover entire surface with a piece of wood cut to fit exactly inside the terrine and weight it evenly with two tea cups, each half filled with water. It is crucial to the formation of a nice, dense terrine that the entire surface be covered and the weight evenly distributed. Place the weighted terrine in the refrigerator for 24 hours.

To prepare poached peaches, combine all ingredients except peaches in a saucepan and bring to a boil. Reduce heat to a simmer and add the peach halves. Simmer until tender, but still firm. Remove peaches from liquid and place in a bowl of ice and water for about 45 seconds. Remove skin from peaches and cut each half into 5 slices, fan shaped.

To prepare salad dressing, whisk together all ingredients except raspberries. Add the raspberries and mix gently. Toss with salad greens just prior to serving.

To serve, place one ½ inch (1 cm) thick slice of foie gras on each of four plates. To one side of the foie gras, place a fan shaped peach.

On the other side of the foie gras, arrange the mixed greens tossed in vinaigrette in an attractive manner. Garnish the plate with chopped chives and sprigs of chervil.

Serves 4

Preparation time is approximately 1½ hours, not including the 24 hours in refrigerator.

Far Left: *Terrine of Foie Gras*

Above: *A Duo of Canadian Venison*

A Duo of Canadian Venison in a Stonechurch Vineyards Cabernet Sauvignon and blueberry jus

4 venison chops
2 venison tenderloins
½ cup (100 mL) venison jus (see method)
2 shallots, chopped
¼ cup (50 mL) Port
½ cup (100 mL) Stonechurch Cabernet Sauvignon
3 tsp (15 mL) Balsamic vinegar
½ pint (250 mL) blueberries
½ cup (100 g) butter
½ cup (100 mL) olive oil
  salt and pepper to taste

VEGETABLES (PEELED AND BLANCHED)

8 baby turnips
12 baby carrots
½ head savoy cabbage, shredded

FOR VENISON JUS

- 2 lbs (1 kg) raw venison bones and trimmings, chopped
- 1½ tbsp (30 mL) olive oil
- 1 carrot, diced
- 1 small onion, diced
- 4 cloves, garlic
- 6 juniper berries
- 1 sprig rosemary
- 1 sprig thyme
- 1 tsp (5 g) tomato paste
- 4¼ cups (1 L) chicken stock
- ⅓ cup (75 mL) Port
- ⅓ cup (75 mL) Stonechurch Cabernet Sauvignon
- ¼ cup (50 mL) cooking brandy
- salt and pepper to taste

Preheat oven to 450F (230C). Roast venison bones and trimmings in a roasting pan with olive oil until brown. Remove pan from oven and strain off the fat. Add carrot, onion, garlic, herbs and juniper berries and return to the oven for another 10 minutes.

Add tomato paste with a wooden spoon and roast for another 5 minutes. Remove pan from oven and transfer the contents to a saucepan. With saucepan on high heat, deglaze the mixture with the Port, Cabernet Sauvignon and brandy. Reduce to half. Add chicken stock and let simmer until reduced to half. Strain through a cheesecloth and season with salt and pepper. For a stronger, more intense sauce, reduce for a little longer.

To prepare the venison sauce, in a saucepan on high heat, saute the shallots in olive oil until golden. Add the Stonechurch Cabernet Sauvignon, Port and Balsamic vinegar. Reduce to ¾. Add the ½ cup (100 mL) of venison jus and bring to a simmer. Strain into a clean saucepan, bring back to a simmer, and slowly stir in ¼ cup (50 g) of butter. Add the blueberries and set aside.

Season the venison chops on both sides with salt and pepper. Brown the chops in a hot skillet with olive oil. Remove and place in a 400F (205°C) oven for 7 minutes or until cooked through. Season the venison tenderloin on both sides with salt and pepper and brown in a skillet, as with the chops. Place in the oven at 400F (205°C) for 5 minutes or until cooked through.

To serve, reheat the blanched turnips and carrots in boiling salted water and toss in a little butter and olive oil. Follow the same procedure with the savoy cabbage.

Cut each tenderloin into about 10 thin slices. Divide the cabbage in four and pile high in the middle of 4 plates. Lean the venison chops on the cabbage and place slices of the tenderloin in a circle next to the chops. Arrange the carrots and turnip attractively on each plate and pour on the venison sauce. Garnish the plates with sprigs of rosemary.

Serves 4

Preparation time is about 1 hour.

Icewine Semifreddo in a buckwheat and pistachio wafer with valhrona chocolate Zabaglione

FOR BUCKWHEAT PISTACHIO WAFER

- ½ cup (55 g) buckwheat flour
- ⅓ cup (40 g) ground almonds
- 2 egg whites
- ¾ cup (120 g) icing sugar
- ¼ cup (50 mL) melted butter
- a pinch of salt
- a dash of vanilla
- 8 pistachios, chopped

FOR SEMIFREDDO

- 5 eggs, separated
- ⅔ cup (150 g) sugar
- 2 cups (500 mL) cream, lightly whipped
- 2 tbsp (30 mL) honey
- 1 cup (250 mL) icewine

Richard and Frances Hunse

FOR VALHRONA CHOCOLATE ZABAGLIONE

- 3 egg yolks
- 1 egg
- ⅓ cup (125 mL) milk
- ⅓ cup (100 mL) Valhrona chocolate, melted
- ¼ cup (50 mL) lightly whipped cream

To prepare buckwheat pistachio wafer, preheat oven to 350F (180°C). Place all ingredients in a bowl and mix with a wooden spoon until smooth. Brush a flat baking pan with melted butter. Refrigerate for 15 minutes.

Spread the batter into medium sized triangles on the baking sheet and bake until golden brown. Remove from oven and form into cups by pressing into a small bowl.

To prepare semifreddo, using a hand mixer, whip egg yolks with ⅓ cup (75 g) of sugar at high speed until pale and fluffy. Set aside.

In a clean bowl, whip egg whites together with the other ⅓ cup (75 g) of sugar until mixture forms soft peaks. Blend yolk mixture with the honey and icewine. Fold in whipped cream, then fold in whites mixture. Spoon into muffin tin or tea cups and freeze overnight. To remove the semifreddo, run hot water over the outside of the cups.

To prepare Valhrona chocolate zabbaglione, whisk together the egg yolks, egg, milk, and melted chocolate in a double boiler until mixture becomes thick and hot. Fold in the whipped cream.

To assemble, place the semifreddo in the buckwheat pistachio cup, serve with the chocolate sauce and the zabbaglione on the side. Garnish the plate with seasonal berries or other fruit.

Serves 4

Preparation time is approximately 45 minutes, but remember that the semifreddo must be frozen overnight.

About the Wines

The Riesling matches well with the Terrine de Foie Gras and the peach and baby green salad. The wine has essences of peach and apricot, and has a clean and crisp finish.

The Cabernet Sauvignon, with an essence of red currants and a lingering taste of black pepper, compliments very well the venison and the sauce.

CHEF MARC THUET

Marc is Executive Chef at Centro Grill and Wine Bar, one of Toronto's finest restaurants. Born in Colmar, Alsace, France, he received his chef training at Lycee Hotelier in Strasbourg, France. Marc worked at several restaurants in France before joining The Dorchester Hotel in London, England.

In Toronto, he worked as a chef at the Toronto Hilton Harbour Castle and the Windsor Arms Hotel before joining Centro's.

A Springtime Dinner on the Escarpment

STONEY RIDGE CELLARS

As soon as you enter the long driveway into Stoney Ridge Cellars at the base of the Niagara Escarpment in Winona, the buzz of farm activity is all around you. There are the sounds of children at play, an old tractor is heading out into the fields, workers in their farm overalls are moving back and forth repairing farm machinery, and baskets and barrels overflowing with fresh fruit are for sale outside the Country Market store. Adjoining the market is the Stoney Ridge wine boutique, an inviting, comfortable shop in which to taste wines and look around. Stoney Ridge offers a number of activities to attract visitors. Apart from a children's play area and the free daily wine tastings, there are also available educational wine seminars, and light lunches as well as the opportunity to buy a variety of Niagara fresh produce.

Stoney Ridge personifies the partnership between Murray Puddicombe, an Ontario grape grower and fruit farmer, and winemaker Jim Warren, a high school teacher and dedicated amateur winemaker of renown. At the beginning, in 1985, Jim initially carried pails of water to a tin shack on the corner of a Niagara Escarpment farm where he produced the first 1,000 gallons of Stoney Ridge wine. Now operating on a farm with 200 acres of vineyards, Stoney Ridge has come a long way in the past few years winning several major international awards including a Gold Medal at VinItaly for their 1990 Eastman Vineyard Chardonnay. Despite being a small winery, Jim Warren produces about 25 VQA varietal wines each year and a number of specialty wines including icewine and exotic blends with names like "Passion", "Romance", and "Jasmine".

Always innovative, Jim has a unique way of financing capital expenditures for the winery. Stoney Ridge ages some of its wine in French oak barrels which are expensive and need to be replaced every five years. For several years now, he has been operating the Stoney Ridge Barrel Club as a way to cover the cost. Forty members each pay a fee every three years which covers the cost of one of the barrels. For their investment each member receives two cases of wine annually, one filled with a limited-edition vintage made exclusively for the club and the other with a vintage of their choice.

Stoney Ridge Cellars is a relaxing place to visit, filled with nostalgia of a time fast disappearing, and Niagara wines of the finest quality.

❧ MENU ❧

Grassberry Salad
Stoney Ridge Gewurztraminer Dry

Braised Stuffed Breast of Veal
Stoney Ridge Merlot Reserve

Lemon Flan
Stoney Ridge Riesling Traminer Icewine

Grassberry Salad

2 lbs (450 g) asparagus
2 qt (2.25 L) strawberries
1 leaf lettuce
1 radicchio

VINAIGRETTE DRESSING
3 cups (750 ml) olive oil
½ cup (125 mL) Gewurztraminer
½ cup (125 mL) vinegar
1 cup (200 g) chopped red onion
3 tsp (15 g) salt
   a pinch of pepper
⅔ cup (150 g) freshly chopped
   herbs, parsley, chervil and chive
¼ cup (50 mL) simple syrup (2 cups
   [450 g] sugar with 4½ cups [1 L]
   water, boiled for 1 minute, then
   removed)

Clean and slice asparagus, blanch and refresh. Clean and cut strawberries into halves or quarters. Combine dressing in-gredients, mixing well (a hand immersor works nicely). Adjust to taste.

Toss vinaigrette with asparagus and strawberries. Serve in a bed of leaf lettuce and radicchio and garnish with chervil.

Serves 6

Preparation time is approximately 20 minutes.

Braised Stuffed Breast of Veal

- 1 veal breast point (purchase from a large butcher shop)
- ⅓ cup (75 g) bacon or smoked pork fat
- 1 tsp (5 g) thyme
- 1 tsp (5 g) marjoram
- ½ tsp (2.5 g) ground garlic
- 2 tsp (10 g) salt
- 2 tsp (10 g) pepper
- 4 cups (1 L) thin Merlot flavored brown sauce

To prepare the stuffing, trim fat, sinew and meat flap from brisket. Double grind or use prepared ground veal. Grind bacon or chop finely and mix well with herbs, salt and pepper.

Pound veal point into square. Spread the stuffing in brisket and roll against grain. Then truss with butcher's twine, dust with flour and shallow fry all sides.

Heat sauce and correct to thick soup consistency. Place in roasting pan with brisket (to cover). Cover the pan and bake at 350F (180°C) for one hour. Let cool in pan, remove and refrigerate overnight.

To serve, bring sauce to the boil and correct. Untruss and slice veal, reheat in sauce and serve. Goes well with red cabbage or brussels sprouts and potato rosti.

Serves 6

Preparation time is approximately 1 hour, but needs to be refrigerated overnight.

Lemon Flan

SWEET PASTRY
- 1¼ cups (300 g) sugar
- 1¼ lb (500 g) shortening
- 2 tsp (10 g) salt
- ¼ cup (50 mL) lemon
- 2 eggs
- ½ cup (120 mL) milk
- 3¾ cups (875 g) pastry flour
  a pinch of baking powder

Cream together sugar, shortening, salt and lemon with a mixer (using paddle attachment). Place eggs in milk, beat and add creamed mixture in two stages. Scrape bowl sides and continue to beat. Sift flour and baking powder and add to mixture beating until smooth. Place dough on floured surface and lightly work dough dry. Refrigerate overnight.

LEMON FILLING

18 eggs
2¼ cups (500 g) sugar
12 lemons zested and juiced
2¼ cups (550 mL) 35% cream

Finger press dough bottom and sides of an 11 inch (27.5 cm) springform pan 2 inches (40 to 50 mm) in thickness with parchment paper. Fill pan with dry beans to maintain wall integrity and bake 10 minutes at 350F (180°C). Remove the beans and continue to bake 10 more minutes or until pastry is golden brown.

To prepare lemon filling, whip together filling ingredients. Check pastry shell for cracks or holes and fill with remaining sweet pastry dough. Pour the filling into shell and bake 300F (150°C) for 1 hour or until top is golden and firm. Let stand for 1 hour and then refrigerate 2 hours before serving.

Serves 10 to 12

Preparation time is about 1 hour, not including the standing and refrigeration time.

CHEF GREG WILLIS

Greg Willis, a native of St. Catharines, Ontario, is a cook by trade and a certified Sommelier. In 1991, he established the Cellar Bench, a winebar in the Old Courthouse in St. Catharines where he features local wines, local micro-brewed beer, and regional fare from farm fresh products.

Greg produces everything from the bread to the complex desserts on the premises, using primarily convection ovens and poaching mediums. The result is comfortable cuisine and the ambience to match.

☙ About the Wines ❧

Chef Greg Willis picked the Gewurztraminer because, he says, "The spice in the wine lends itself to the flavour of the asparagus and elevates the complexity. The acid of the strawberries and vinaigrette lower the perceived acidity of the wine."

In choosing the Merlot Reserve with the veal, Greg explains that the deep cherry flavours of the Merlot accent the light meat and hold up well with the sauce.

For the dessert, he says, "The intense lemon flavour of the flan and the sweetness balance themselves perfectly with the icewine, and the apricot aroma stays forward."

Above: *Murray Paddicombe and Jim Warren.*

A Romantic Dinner with Friends

VINELAND ESTATE WINES

I t's one of the most picturesque wineries in Niagara. A 150-year old homestead nestled at the base of a steep part of the Niagara Escarpment and surrounded by 75 acres of rolling vineyards and a view of Lake Ontario far below, Vineland Estates leaves visitors with an unforgettable memory of both the beauty of nature and of Vineland's excellent wines.

The winery is owned by John Howard, who lives in a castle he built just down the gravel road from the winery, and is affectionately known as Castle Howard by neighbours. Formerly a senior executive of a major North American corporation, he used to buy the award winning Rieslings and Icewines produced at Vineland Estates to take as gifts during his extensive travels around the world. When he was approached in 1991 by Herman Weis, the former owner and a well known European winemaker, he decided he liked the product so much he would buy the winery. Herman Weis had originally purchased the old Mennonite farm in 1979 and planted superior *vitis vinifera* vines. He established Vineland Estates in 1984.

Using his extensive international marketing experience, John's long term goal is to help make Vineland Estates and the Niagara Wine Region a tourist destination similar to the Napa and Sonoma Valleys in California.

He is well on his way to achieving his goal with world class wines produced by Allan Schmidt, Vineland Estates' general manager and winemaker. Allan is a third generation winemaker from British Columbia's Okanagan Valley—his grandfather emigrated from Germany. Allan studied cold climate vine growing and European winemaking technology in the Nahe Region of Germany and worked at Heitz Cellars in California before moving back to British Columbia as winemaker at their Sumac Ridge family winery. When he had a chance to take control of Vineland Estates in 1986, he headed East.

Allan loves winter camping, so much so that he and his brother Brian, the Cellar Master at the winery, have been to the Magnetic North Pole by dog sled. They took along some Vineland Estate Icewine to test the ageing effect of arctic travel and the magnetic polarization of the Pole on

Left: *Winemaker Allan Schmidt*

Right: *Overlooking the vineyards from the Vineland Estate deck.*

the fermented grape. It turns out that when they returned the bouquet on the Icewine was much creamier and tasted a year older than the same Icewine not on the trip. It was also a little softer and less acidic. They plan further research through other trips to the Pole and invite fellow wine lovers to join them.

Before joining Vineland, Allan already had an affinity with the winery which has built its success on Riesling wines. Riesling has traditionally constituted about 80 per cent of the winery's product portfolio, although the winery has also won international awards for its Icewine, Chardonnay and Pinot Noir. Allan's loyalty to Riesling comes from his belief that it is the best grape to work with because it provides such a range of possible styles. Indigenous to the cooler regions of Germany and Alsace, it is characteristically known as a fresh, crisp wine when produced in a classic dry style. According to Allan, Vineland Estates' unmistakable well balanced backbone of acidity in their Niagara Bench Rieslings maintains longevity in great Rieslings and Gewurztraminers.

There is no better way to spend a beautiful afternoon than with a glass of St. Urban Vineyard Riesling on Vineland's winedeck and patio overlooking the vineyards, and feasting on a selection of their world famous cheeses, assorted patés, smoked salmon and bagels, soft Bavarian pretzels and fresh garden salads. There's an adjacent historic carriage house which features art auctions, craft shows and monthly theme dinners. And if you get the urge to stay the evening, there's a cottage across the lane which has been converted into a cozy Bed and Breakfast.

❧ MENU ❧

Soup from Butternut Squash with Smoked Whitefish, Ravioli and Pelee Gold Whitefish Caviar
Vineland Estates 1990 Semi-Dry Riesling

Warm Salad from Pork Cheek, Lentils and Garden Greens with crisp Marjoram Potatoes
Vineland Estates 1992 Estate Chardonnay

Lemon Foam with Wild Ontario Blueberry Compote and Hazelmaple Twile
Vineland Estates 1992 Vidal Icewine

Soup from Butternut Squash with Smoked Whitefish, Ravioli and Pelee Gold Whitefish Caviar

1 medium size butternut squash
2 onions
1 bunch of green onion
1 cup (250 mL) dry Riesling
2 tbsp (40 g) butter
1 tbsp (20 mL) sour cream
¼ cup (50 mL) cream (35%)
⅓ bunch Italian parsley
3 cups (750 mL) chicken stock
¼ lb (100 g) smoked whitefish
2 tbsp (40 g) Pelee Gold whitefish caviar
1 bayleaf, 6 juniper berries, 1 twig of thyme
  touch nutmeg, salt and pepper
⅓ cup (100 g) pasta dough

For soup, peel and slice onions. Saute in butter without taking colour and add cut up squash. Deglaze with Riesling, add chicken stock to the boil and then add bay leaf, juniper berries, and thyme. Allow to boil for approximately ½ hour then put in food processor and strain through fine strainer. Keep aside.

To prepare ravioli, take out all bones from whitefish and break into small pieces. Add sour cream and fine sliced green onions. Roll out the pasta dough and make ravioli as usual.

To serve, put ravioli in boiling water for about 3 minutes. Meanwhile, heat up the soup and add whipped cream, fine chopped parsley, nutmeg and salt and pepper to taste. Put soup in a bowl, ravioli on top and at the last moment put the whitefish caviar on top of the ravioli.

Serves 6

Preparation time is approximately 45 minutes.

Cook pork cheek with 2 onions, bayleaves, cloves, juniper berries, salt, thyme, peppercorns in a pot with just enough water to cover for 1½ hours. After that time, take porkcheek out and remove as much fat and skin as possible.

Slice up 2 onions and sauté in olive oil, then add soaked lentils to pork stock and bring to a boil. Cook until lentils are tender. While lentils are still warm add mustard, vinegar, olive oil and then let sit at least 1½ hours before serving.

Above: *Former owner Hermann Weis and his daughter, Anne, with John Hall and his daughter, Erin*

Below: *Soup from Butternut Squash with Smoked Whitefish, Ravioli and Pelee Gold Whitefish Caviar*

Warm Salad from Pork Cheek, Lentils and Garden Greens with Crisp Marjoram Potatoes

- 1 pork cheek (purchase from butcher)
- ⅔ cup (150 g) lentils
- 5 onions
- 2 leeks
- 4 shallots
  garden greens by season
- 2 tbsp (40 g) grain mustard
- 3 Yukon gold potatoes
- 1 bunch of marjoram
- 2 tbsp (40 g) butter
- ⅓ cup (75 mL) olive oil
- ¼ cup (50 mL) apple cider vinegar
- 3 bayleaves, 4 cloves, 5 juniper berries
- 1 twig of thyme, pepper corns, salt

To serve, peel potatoes and slice very thin, then fry with marjoram, onion, salt and pepper. Put in the oven until crisp. Arrange salad greens on the plate, add chopped up shallots to lentils and heat up pork cheek in remaining pork stock with sliced up leeks.

When pork cheek is hot, slice it and arrange on salad green with lentils and leeks.

Serves 6

In preparing this dish, you need to allow for initial cooking time of 1½ hours and a sitting time of about 1½ hours. The actual preparation time is approximately 1 hour.

Lemon Foam with Wild Ontario Blueberry Compote and Hazelmaple Tuile

FOR MOUSSE
- 3 lemons
- ⅓ cup (80 g) sugar
- 1 cup (250 mL) whipping cream
- 4 eggs
- 1 sheet of gelatin
- ½ tbsp (10 mL) sour cream

FOR COMPOTE
- ½ pint (300 g) wild Ontario blueberries
- ⅓ cup (75 mL) of dry Riesling
- ⅓ cup (80 g) sugar

FOR TUILE
- ½ cup (90 g) maple sugar
- ½ cup (60 g) pastry flour
- ¼ cup (50 mL) melted butter
- 2 egg whites
- ¾ cup (100 g) finely chopped hazelnuts

Take zest of 1 lemon and all of its juice, 4 egg yolks and 2 tbsp (40 g) of sugar and whisk over steaming water until nice and foamy. (Be careful. Don't whisk too hot or you'll get scrambled egg). Add the soaked gelatin sheet.

Whip the cream and egg whites with the other half of the sugar. When lemon mixture is almost cold, fold in the whipping cream and egg whites. Add the sour cream and let mixture cool. Put in refrigerator for at least 2 to 3 hours.

To prepare the compote, put half of blueberries, white wine and sugar into pot and cook until ⅓ is remaining. Put in blender and then strain back

into pot, bring to a boil and add the other half of the blueberries. Once it has reached a boil, remove from heat and cool.

For tuile, mix all ingredients together. Then spread on tray very thinly and bake at 425F (220°C) until golden brown. Immediately remove from the tray with spatula and form over cup.

Serves 6

Preparation time is about 1 hour, but allow 2 to 3 hours to let stand in refrigerator.

Opposite page, far left: *Warm Salad from Porkcheek, Lentils and Garden Greens with Crisp Marjoram Potatoes*
Opposite page above: *Lemon foam with Wild Ontario Blueberry Composte and Hazelmaple Tuile*
Above: *Chef Michael Stadtlander*

CHEF MICHAEL STADTLANDER

Known as one of Canada's premier chefs, Michael is a restless experimenter in finding new ways to bring out the very best flavours in local produce and game. Before emigrating to Canada in 1980, he served an apprenticeship in Germany, Switzerland and Germany. In Toronto he opened Scaramouche with Jamie Kennedy, later opened Stadtlander's and after spending time travelling in Europe, started Nekah in Toronto in 1988.

Michael and his wife, Nobuyo, have opened the 100 acre Eigensinn Farm which is located about two hours north of Toronto where they provide a multi-course dinner and bed and breakfast as well as meeting and conference facilities, catering, special event dinners and cooking classes. Michael also has a cooking school for young chefs.

Michael says their aim is to be organically self-sufficient raising their own livestock and growing their own grain, vegetables and fruit. They want to feature the best from their surroundings in the tradition of Old Ontario, but with a decidedly modern approach.

About the Wines

Michael Stadtlander picked the 1990 Semi Dry Riesling with the soup because of the balance between the crispness and fruitiness of the Riesling and the flavour of the butternut squash. The acidity of the wine works well with the smoked fish. According to Michael, "the wine and the many flavours of the food in this dish work in harmony."

He chose the 1992 Estate Chardonnay because, "its crispness offsets the meaty flavour of the porkcheek and balances well with the lentils and garden greens."

The dominant peach and apricot flavours of the 1992 Vidal Icewine complement nicely the lemon foam and blueberry compote of the dessert.

Andy Brandt

As Chair and Chief Executive Officer of the Liquor Control Board of Ontario, Andy Brandt does not have much time to spend in the kitchen. But he loves to swap recipes with his friends and colleagues and, when he can, to try them out.

The affable head of the LCBO is responsible for the largest buyer and retailer of beverage alcohol products in the world, with more than 3,000 wines, spirits and beers available in more than 600 stores. A provincial government enterprise, with annual sales of approximately $2 billion, the LCBO employs, counting part-time workers, some 4,500 people.

Before his appointment to the LCBO, Andy Brandt had a long and distinguished career in public service. He served on the Council for the City of Sarnia, Ontario for almost a decade, including three terms as Mayor. In

1981, he was elected to the Ontario Legislative Assembly as Member of Provincial Parliament for Sarnia. At the Ontario Legislature, he served as Parliamentary Assistant to the Minister of Labour, Minister of the Environment, Minister of Industry and Trade, and as Leader of the Ontario Progressive Conservative Party.

Over the years, he has also played a very active role in numerous community organizations and has been recognized for "outstanding community service" by the Rotary Club. Born in London, Ontario he and his wife, Patricia, now live in Sarnia. They have two daughters, Sheree and Lori, two grandsons, Jamie and Kyle and two granddaughters, Jessie and Karli Loren.

Andy's spaghetti sauce recipe, which is legendary in political circles, has been in the family for a long time. Since it can be frozen, it's ideal for a quick dinner when family or friends drop in for an unexpected visit.

About the Wines

Two full-bodied wines that match well with Andy's spaghetti sauce with meatballs are Henry of Pelham Estates Baco Noir and Chateau des Charmes Cabernet Sauvignon.

Spaghetti Sauce with Meatballs

FOR THE SAUCE:

- 2 x 28 oz (800 g) cans of tomatoes
- 1 small can of tomato paste
- 3 bay leaves
- ¼ cup (50 g) each, chopped green and red peppers
- 1 chopped celery stalk
- 3 chopped garlic cloves
- 1 small chopped onion
- ¾ tsp (4 g) crushed chilies
- ¾ tsp (4 g) tarragon
- 1 tsp (5 g) ground parsley
- ¾ tsp (4 g) oregano
- 1 tsp (5 g) sweet basil
- 1 tsp (5 g) celery salt
- 1½ tsp (7.5 g) chili powder

FOR MEATBALLS:

- 1½ lb (675 g) ground meat mixture of beef, pork, veal
- ½ cup (100 g) of breadcrumbs
- 1 egg, beaten
- 1 tsp (5 g) basil
- 1 tsp (5 g) garlic powder
- 1 tsp (5 g) parsley
- 1 tsp (5 g) celery salt
- ½ tsp (2.5 g) poultry seasoning
- 1 tsp (5 g) chili powder
- ½ tsp (2.5 g) crushed chilies
  vegetable oil for frying

Simmer tomatoes, tomato paste and bay leaves for one hour. Sauté peppers, celery, garlic cloves and onion in ⅓ cup (75 mL) of vegetable oil until soft. Add drained vegetables to tomato sauce, reserving oil. Add remaining spices, mix and simmer.

Combine meat, ½ of breadcrumbs and remaining meatball ingredients. Shape into balls and roll in remaining breadcrumbs. Fry in oil until browned, and drain. Add to sauce and simmer for 3 hours.

Serves Preparation time, not including the simmering time of 4 hours, is about 40 minutes.

TASTING FOOD WITH WINE

There are some simple guidelines which will help you to enjoy particular pairings of food and wine. Always balance the weight of the food with the weight of the wine. For example, a rich Chardonnay works better with equally rich food such as salmon or lobster. A crisp, dry Riesling requires a lighter dish. Always match your wine to the strongest flavour on the plate. For desserts, always keep the dessert less sweet than the dessert wine.

With Pinot Noir
Beef, duck, turkey, veal, and other smoked meats and poultry.
Earthy, rich flavours such as caramelized onions, mushrooms, and tomatoes.
Mild cheeses.

With Cabernet Sauvignon
Quail, lamb, duck.
Pungent herbs and spices like rosemary, garlic and pepper-corns.
Soft ripening cheeses such as Camembert and Brie.
Hard grating cheeses like Romano and Parmesan.

With Chardonnay
Duck, pheasant, veal, quail, and other full-flavoured poultry and meats.
Salmon, trout, scallops, and other rich seafood.
Aromatic herbs such as basil, dill and roasted garlic.

With Seyval Blanc
Seafood such as bass, sole, mussels, and clams.
Grilled cuts of chicken or pork.
Olives, roasted peppers.

With Merlot

Full flavoured meats and poultry such as lamb, duck, quail, and rabbit.
Rich flavoured vegetables and pungent herbs.
Spices like nutmeg.
Soft ripening cheeses.

Icewine

The Niagara wine industry is world renowned for its icewine which has won numerous international awards and has become a major export item, particularly to Japan and the United States. The weather conditions are ideal for producing this nectar in the Niagara Region because the grapes must be left on the vines to freeze solid. Temperatures must drop to at least -7 degrees Celsius before the grapes can be harvested, which is usually between January and February. While the berries are frozen, small amounts of concentrated juice is pressed out. The juice is very sweet and high in acidity.

The thick skinned Riesling and Vidal grape varieties make the best icewine. Tasting icewine, which makes a great dessert on its own, is definitely a unique and necessary experience.

Some Wine Terms

(Used with permission of Ontario Wine Council)

Acidity: The agreeable sharp taste caused by natural fruit acids.

Brut: French term designating driest grade of Champagne or sparkling wine.

Character: The combination of taste, bouquet and colour in a wine.

Cooperage: General term used to designate containers in which wines are stored and aged, and includes casks and wooden or stainless steel ageing tanks.

Estate-Bottled: Wine that was produced and bottled on a property controlled by the winery.

Fermentation: A process whereby yeasts interact with sugars to produce alcohol and carbon dioxide. Through such a process, grape juice is transformed into wine.

Flowery: A term denoting the fragrance of blossoms in a wine's bouquet or aroma.

Fortified Wine: Wine such as a sherry, port and muscatel to which alcohol has been added, usually in the form of brandy or grape spirit, to increase their alcoholic content.

Fruity: Term applied to a fine young wine which has the aroma and flavour of fresh fruit.

Full: Pleasingly strong in flavour, bouquet or taste.

Maturity: A state reached by wine through ageing.

Nose: Professional winetaster term describing quality of bouquet.

Rounded: A complimentary term for a wine whose qualities are in balance.

Soft: Term describing the pleasant smoothness of wines of low astringency, and not related to sweetness.

Table Wine: A wine with a maximum of 14 per cent alcohol by volume.

Tart: The sharp, astringent taste of fruit acid. When present in a moderate degree, tartness lends a pleasant freshness to a wine.

Tawny: The brownish-red colour acquired by some red wines in ageing. The characteristic of Tawny Port.

Tannin: An astringent acid found to some degree in all wine, but more in red than in white. The proper degree of tannic acid is essential to aged, high quality red wines while an excess can ruin a wine.

Varietal: The wine name taken from the grape variety used to produce it. Varietal names include: Chardonnay, Riesling, Marechal Foch.

Vinifera: The most important of the 32 species of vines making up the genus *Vitis* in the botanical classification. *Vitis vinifera* is the species of grape from which all the wines of Europe are made.

Vinifera Hybrid: A cross between the Labrusca and the vinifera families and used in many of Canada's premium wines.

Vinification: A broad term covering the whole process of turning grapes into wine, except for the vineyard operations. It includes fermentation, clarification and ageing.

Vintage: The harvesting, crushing and fermentation of grapes into wine. This term is also applied to the crop of grapes or the wine for one season.

Vintner: Includes, for example, wine growers and wine makers.

Viticulture: The cultivation of the vine, also the science of grape production.

Some Cooking Terms

Al Dente: Cooked until barely tender, but not soft.

Blanch: To immerse food in boiling water for a short time.

Caramelize: Cooking sugar and water together will result in them turning a golden brown, or caramelizing. Natural sugars in such vegetables as carrots will do the same during cooking.

Deglaze: During sauteing there are small brown bits that are created that are often used in making a sauce more flavourful. This term refers to adding water or wine to a pan to dissolve these bits.

Glaze: Give food a shiny coating of sauce before serving.

Hull: Refers to the outer covering of a fruit.

Incorporate: To combine or blend thoroughly.

Reduce: To decrease liquid in a pan by boiling it over high heat.

Roux: A cooked mixture of flour and a fat used as a thickener in a sauce or soup.

Sachet: A small pouch or bag used to contain herbs.

Sweat: Consists of putting buttered parchment paper on top of vegetables in a pan, covering the pan with a lid, and letting them cook until softened.

Translucent: Cooking until clear or transparent.

Whisk: Used to beat ingredients until combined.

Zest: It is the coloured rind of citrus fruit and is normally grated or cut into thin slivers.

Credits

Editor: Jackie Lealess
Jacket Design: Dave Hader
Text Design: Jacquline Hope Raynor
Photography: Dieter Hessel
Wine Consultant: Ian Ophile
Digital Colour & Film: Linotext
Printing: Metropole Litho
Publisher: Nick Pitt